The Amiras

Lords of Ottoman Armenia

Pascal Carmont

Translated from French into English by
Marika Blandin

Preface by
Bernard Dorin, French Ambassador

Taderon Press
London

This publication has been made possible with a generous grant from the Calouste Gulbenkian Foundation.

The Amiras: Lords of Ottoman Armenia is an English translation of *Les Amiras: Seigneurs de l'Arménie ottomane* by Pascal Carmont with a preface by Bernard Dorin (Paris: Editions Salvator, 1999). The English translation was made by Marika Blandin and edited by Nora Vosbigian.

ISBN 978-1-903656-35-8

Published by Taderon Press by special arrangement with the Gomidas Institute.

For further information please contact:
Gomidas Institute
42 Blythe Rd.
London, W14 0HA
ENGLAND
Email: *info@gomidas.org*
Web: *www.gomidas.org*

To the memory of my grandmother, to whom I owe the knowledge of the history and language of my ancestors.

TABLE OF CONTENTS

Preface

Armenia, Armenia... as far back as I can remember, Armenia has been curiously present and familiar in my life. In my sick room as a child my parents fought the miasma by burning small pieces of scented paper called "papier d'Arménie" whose light smoke I inhaled with delight. Later in life, the word Armenia evoked the Orient, pomp, wealth, mystery, adventure. My first Armenia was imaginary and romantic.

My second encounter with Armenia was "the red poster." I was still a child but already ardently patriotic. My gaze fixed on those faces swollen by torture whose names were Armenian. Those who the Nazis called "terrorists" had fought for my country and had given their lives for it. A surge of infinite gratitude went out to those tortured men.

The real Armenia, at least the small part that still remained beyond the Arax, I came to know much later, in 1969, when I accompanied the French Minister Robert Galley, whose diplomatic counsellor I was, to the Transcauscasian Republic of the U.S.S.R. Tired of visiting shoe-factories, we asked and finally obtained permission to see a religious monument. Our Soviet hosts led us to a small church with a delightfully carved stone cross, whose monks, we were told, had fled a Persian incursion in the 12th century and had taken refuge in the West. I was surprised and moved to observe that the plan of this church was the same, but much smaller, as the Romanesque collegiate church of Saint Amant De Boixe, in my region of Angoulême, where I was to get married two years later; an astonishing example of the Occident being inspired by the Orient. Near Yerevan, where we admired the splendid illuminations of Armenian manuscripts at the National Library, there was a "Monument to Genocide," where the names of lost Armenian provinces were engraved. I remember it as a large white arrow leaning towards ancient Armenia in Turkey, like an accusing finger or a reproach. From there one could see Mount Ararat, that of Noah's Ark, in a blue haze...

If I have recalled at length my encounters with Armenia it is because they have helped me to understand "inwardly," if I can put it thus, the admirable book by Pascal Carmont which I should now like to present after saying a few words concerning the author.

I first came to know Pascal Carmont, whom René Gousset pointed out as *"the hope of the Armenian history of tomorrow"*, at the end of the seventies, during a journey to Mozambique, where he worked for the French Embassy, and later, better still, when he became my Consul-Général in Johannesburg. I have kept a dazzling memory of this latter period.

Pascal Carmont is a very cultivated man with a culture bestowed by a very long family and national tradition. In his case, this culture is never conceited or arrogant; on the contrary, it seems to flow naturally like a modest mountain stream of his ancestral lands. This modesty is so particular to the author that one is really struck by it. It is, in fact, a mark of his immense talent and great ambition, as he makes his country of origin known to others with utmost respect for its most authentic and sometimes lesser known characteristics. I would also like to commend Pascal Carmont's loyalty to France, his country of adoption, all the more dear to him because he chose it freely.

But no doubt it is subtlety that best characterizes the author of this book. I was able to observe this at leisure in his diplomatic work in South Africa where his reports on people, situations and events were so insightful. And it is the same subtle analysis that I rediscovered with great pleasure in his work on the Armenia of the Amiras. I should now like to refer to this work.

To start with, one reads the book without stopping. If the comparison were not a well worn one, I would be tempted to say "like a novel." And in a certain way it is indeed a novel, that of a historical adventure, and so astonishing, that one might think it was "romanticized," were it not based on documents and unquestionable facts. However that may be, the style is light, fluid, always pleasant and sometimes with a touch of precocity which evokes the Orient. As for the anecdotes, numerous, entertaining and generally full of humour, they contribute to his account of truth and authenticity which charms one naturally. The book is, therefore, a "distraction" in the literal meaning of the work, that is to say, something that removes you from day-to-day reality and plunges you into the Turkey of another age, so different from to-day. In this respect one cannot but feel a deep admiration for the glory of Armenian nobles, the Amiras, who illuminated Turkey for generations, and might have been forgotten were it not for this beautiful and great book.

To be more precise, it is a work of memory, and for Armenia, it is essential to remember. Pascal Carmont has had the merit and courage not to obscure the tragic end of Ottoman Armenia, already beginning with the bloody persecutions of Abdul-Hamid, the "red sultan," and completed after the Young Turk revolution by the first great genocide of the 20th century. It is distressing to note that it is the "French idea," shockingly perverted, of a nation state, which led to the elimination of Ottoman national minorities, Greeks in the coastal regions and Armenians in the interior.

Even to-day this disastrous conception leads to the bloody repression of the Kurdish uprising in Turkey which has already resulted in many thousands of deaths, absurd destruction, and millions of refugees. More than thirty years ago a leading Turk declared to my friend Emir Nedir Khan: if they rebel we will do to the people of Ere[*] "what we did to the people of Ayo."[†]

Turkey is a great noble country, heir to a great culture with a glorious history. Why do its present leaders not understand that it would be in their interest to reject the atrocious heritage of Talaat Pasha? A state becomes greater by recognizing its errors and, like the Jews, the Armenians have a right to the recognition of their national ordeals and to apologies. Similarly, how can the Turkey of to-day hope to be a member, as wished by others, of our European Union, as long as it pursues its military operations against its own Kurdish citizens called "terrorists" for the needs of a bad cause? We, who admire Turkey, can but entreat it, in its own interest, to follow an entirely different path.

But apart from the particularly attractive character of this book, apart from its historical interest, what seems to me most important are the lessons we can learn for the Europe of to-day. We can see a Muslim empire considered by the Occident as fanatical and uncompromising, which not only recognized its national and religious minorities – the two notions often being confounded – but also granted them a status and privileges which placed them apart and sometimes even in a position to practically manage the affairs of the empire. We can see a Sultan considered as a terrible despot, in addition a Caliph, that is to say "assistant" and successor of the Prophet, Commander of the Faithful, surround himself with Jews and Christians, Greeks and Armenians, to help and advise him. Thus it was that in Ottoman Turkey this very "modern" notion of real "nations" existed – admittedly without delimited territories of their own – but whose subjects had a personal status which respected their beliefs, languages, and national

---

* Ere *(Kurdish)*: Yes.

† Ayo *(Armenian)*: Yes.

traditions. What an extraordinary example of tolerance that Turkey gave us, the same that Pascal Carmont allows us to discover!

A descendant of a great Armenian family, a loyal and passionate servant of the French State, who inwardly maintains the fullness of his Armenian identity, as does his exemplary wife who has supported him admirably throughout his career; is Pascal Carmont not the most accomplished of Amiras?

May readers now be carried away by his imagination to the shores of the Bosphorus; let them glide on the waters aboard a caique ready to take them back in time and abandon themselves to the nostalgia of things that have been and will never be again....

Bernard Dorin
French Ambassador
[Paris, 1999]

Preamble

Paris, July 1935

I was seven years old. It was early morning and promised to be a lovely summer's day. We were preparing – my mother, my aunt and I – to have breakfast when the doorbell rang. A special postman brought us an invitation from Princess Malcom Khan and her three daughters to come to tea that same afternoon.

The Princess, over 90 years old, was the widow of the famous Persian Ambassador to London and Rome and the eldest daughter of Arakel Bey Dadian. Her family had given Turkey a dynasty of great masters of armaments and her youngest daughter, born in London, was the god daughter of Queen Victoria and bore her name.

My aunt didn't lose a moment. Being very respectful of etiquette, she told me – while my mother watched amused – in the peremptory tone she knew so well, "Artine,* we must set ourselves to work. You are going to learn how to kiss her hand."

At seven, I didn't really understand what was happening. I was slightly worried but, being a docile little boy, I tried to do what I was asked.

Aunt Herminé was in her element. Very "Grand Siecle" in her dressing-gown, she began by imitating the Princess' welcome and recreating it in an unchanging setting. "'Oh what a lovely child!' 'How he has grown!' 'He's adorable!' And when she'll say these words, you should kiss her hand."

Suiting the action to the word and the perfection to the action, my aunt initiated me in the most elegant rite of masculine *savoir-vivre*; she taught me with accomplished artistry how to lean forward, the deep head-bow, and the delicate homage of lips lightly brushing the venerable hand.

It was time to leave. It would be an understatement to say I wasn't nervous. On our arrival I saw the Princess surrounded by her daughters and she gave me a kindly smile. Very upright, clad in a sumptuous pink brocade gown touching the floor, her neck adorned with a pearl necklace of the same colour falling to her waist, she had a royal appearance which no doubt my childish admiration enhanced. Fortunately I carried out my mission

* Armenian version of Pascal.

correctly, under the touched looks of my family and flattering ones of the ladies, including our cousin Anna Boutros-Ghali who, at that time, was mourning for her husband Naguib Pasha.

I was invited to sit down in an armchair. Suddenly I saw the princess cross the drawing-room, tottering because of her great age, as she approached me. She sat beside me and, applauded by her daughters, recited by heart *"Le Corbeau et Le Renard."*

Such was my first "official" contact with this world which was mine.

Lastingly marked by this aristocratic experience, I dreamt only of nobility, to the point of making it the major subject of my conversations with my grandmother who, one day, finally said, "Listen, Artine, we too are nobles; we are descendants of the Amiras." This small remark had a decisive effect on me and resulted in my conversion to forever worship my ancestors.

The family surroundings did the rest. I grew up among the last descendants of the Amiras, personalities both distinguished and ruined, whom my grandmother often received. Each of them told me their history. Very soon I felt I was the bearer of a message which would be lost unless I revived and restored it to the annals of history. I do not intend this book to be a scholarly work but a personal memoir, blending the legendary with the authentic.

For 150 years the Amiras were, in the Ottoman Empire, the shadow dignitaries, the exclusive magnates of the Turkish world. Members of a minority, they imposed themselves, despite their duality as Armenians and Christians, on the immense Turkish Muslim Empire, and their influence lasted from the start of the 18th century to the middle of the 19th century.

Today this power is forgotten, probably as much by Turks as by Armenians. Yet here lies the only agreement which, tacitly, still exists between these two hostile peoples: a mutual forgetting of a common past.

Present day Turkish policy has dictated that everything should be done to "conjure away" Armenia, thus turning its back on a past which should not be remembered. Genocide has come between past and present, and here we approach the taboo of the relationship between Armenia and Turkey. In 1915 the Turks annihilated Ottoman Armenia. Since then the executioners have not cast off their mask of innocence so that the very mention of Turkey echoes in Armenian ears as the synonym of absolute evil. Nevertheless, it is important to rethink the genocide, not only to cease "brooding over a past of disaster,"* but also to obtain, above all, its recognition and a formal confession of the truth.

Independently of the abuses of Ottoman domination, the Armeno-Turkish relationship prior to the late Ottoman period had nothing in common with the terror of the Hamidian era or the brutality of the Young Turks. Before these latter horrors, there was some harmony and an enduring understanding during which the Amiras played an important part in Ottoman affairs, as much by their defiance as by their power.

It would be a serious mistake to omit from Armenia's past one of the most interesting components of its history which some experts say constituted a most remarkable period. I consider this account is less of an Armenia conquered by Turkey than that of a Turkey impregnated by Armenia.

With regards to the aristocrats of Ottoman Armenia who exerted such influence on Turkey, it would be wrong to ignore what Turkey owes to Armenia and worse to allow four hundred years of co-existence to be effaced by twenty years of madness.

---

* The word is that of Gerard Chaliand.

Map Showing Historic Armenia and the Ottoman Empire cir. 18th century, with an outline of the Armenian Republic and Artsakh today.

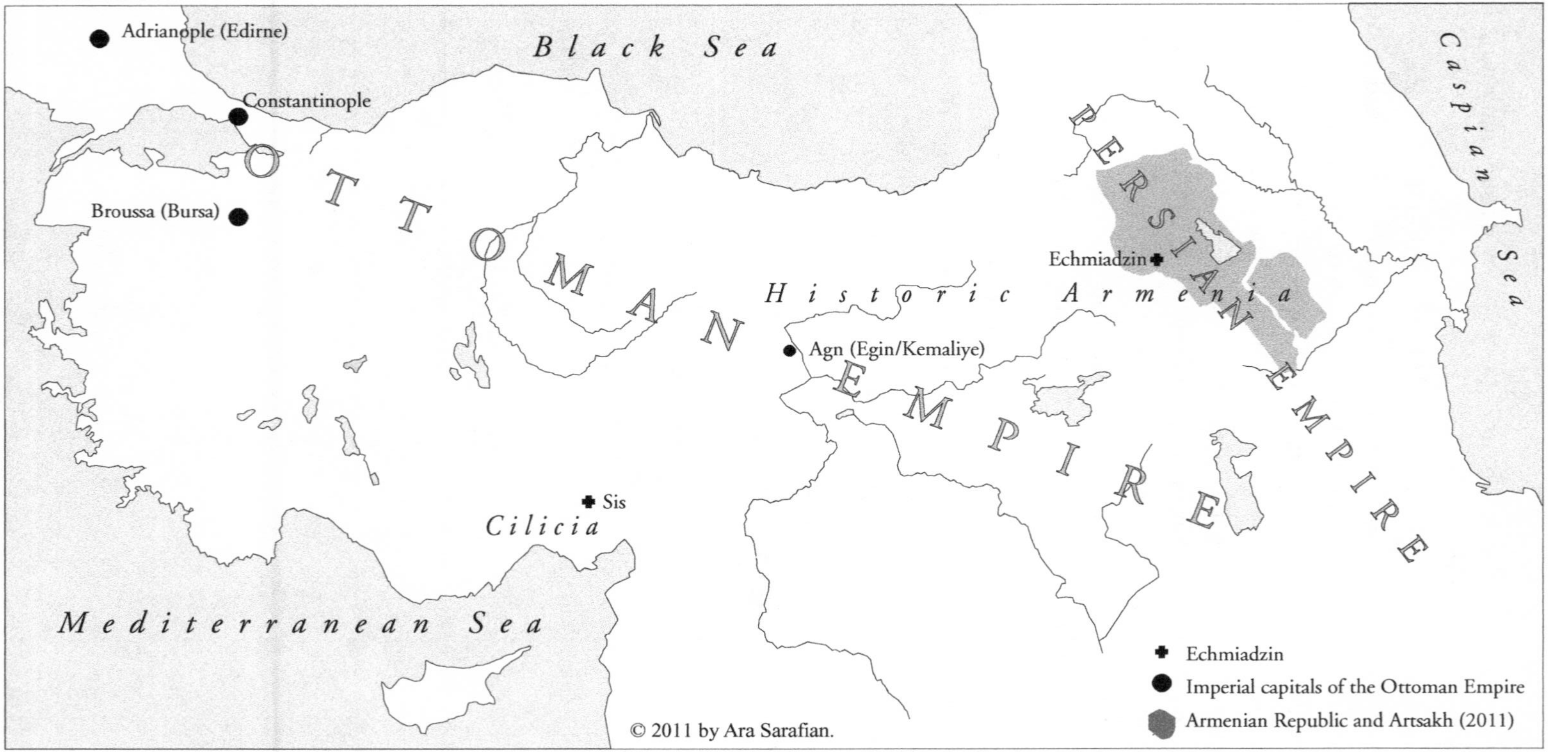

Adrianople (Edirne)
Black Sea
Constantinople
Broussa (Bursa)
OTTOMAN EMPIRE
Historic Armenia
PERSIAN EMPIRE
Caspian Sea
Echmiadzin
Agn (Egin/Kemaliye)
Sis
Cilicia
Mediterranean Sea

Echmiadzin
Imperial capitals of the Ottoman Empire
Armenian Republic and Artsakh (2011)

I

Armenia Before the Ottoman Conquest

Armenia is a county with a strange destiny. Its people, dating back nearly three thousand years, is one of the most ancient in the world, whereas so many other ancient nations have disappeared from the face of the earth.

Armenians have always manifested an astonishing vitality, which has enabled them to overcome two major obstacles: firstly, the vulnerability of their geographical position, and secondly, the individuality of their character. Division was more profitable to petty kings than uniting against an enemy for the integrity of the realm!

Thus, while scoffing at the world from the heights of the Caucasus, Armenia remained a fragile land, contended for by the great empires to its east and the west – Roman, Persian, Byzantine, Arab, and Turkish. Armenia's history is that of alternating periods of independence and subjection, the second being longer than the first.

The survival of Armenia is due less to the relatively modest number of Armenians than to their unwavering passion for cultivating and defending their national identity. And it is such a continuing duality that has nourished Armenia with an unquestionable paradox between the appeals of individualism and devotion to their nation, between the radiance of their intelligence and the yoke of their rashness.

To the credit of their intelligence one must put the proverbial richness of their language, which gave rise to a flourishing literature dominated by remarkable religious men and great mystics.

Their sanctuaries, in particular, include as many architectural treasures as patriotic ones. These spiritual shields of the nation have radiated their magnificence all over the world.

Indeed, their church, rightly proud of its admirable liturgy, embodies better than anything their persistence to save their national identity.

So, what are the origins of Armenians? They are related to the Thraceo-Phrygians and coming from the northern shores of Pont Euxin (Black Sea), their ancestors crossed the Bosphorus towards the end of the second millennium B.C. going eastwards and incorporating the powerful kingdom of Urartu which included the eastern provinces of modern Turkey and the north-west of Iran. This kingdom gave its name to Mount Ararat situated at the eastern extremity of Turkey, the mythical mountain of Armenians, 5,165 metres in height, on whose summit Noah's Ark was said to have landed as the flood subsided.

Urartu completes its armenisation at the end of the 7th century B.C. and is, perhaps, the legendary kingdom founded by the equally legendary Hayg, who was supposed to have given the country the Armenian version of its name, *Hayasdan,* or country of the Hays. It is a mystery why the rest of the world has designated the "Hay" people as "Armenian," and this, since approximately 520 B.C. It was then that the Emperor Darius I of Persia had engraved in cuneiform writing, on the great inscription of Behistoun, the names of the vassal nations of his empire, including "Arminiya" and "Armina" as being respectively Armenia and the Armenians.

At about the same time, the Greek historians also began to mention the "Armenoi," while a century later, in 401, Xenophon had the opportunity of studying their country after receiving shelter from them during the retreat of the Ten Thousand.

In the Armenian language there is no trace of "Armenia" except for the male name of Armen and the female Armenouhi, as well as the name of Armavir, the first capital of the country.

In the 6th century B.C. (c. 590-547) Armenia was dominated by the Medes before being incorporated, for two centuries, in the great empire of the Achemenide Persians (c. 547-331), where it formed a semi-autonomous satrapy. The political and cultural influence of Iran left its mark on Armenians.

From the end of the 6th century B.C. – that is to say around the year 500 – this satrapy was governed by the Orontides family (in Armenian Yervantouni), the first Armenian dynasty sufficiently powerful to strike its own coinage and to free itself from Persian "protection" thanks to the victory of Alexander the Great over Darius III (331).

While maintaining its autonomous status, Armenia, from the end of the fourth century B.C. to the start of the second, was under the suzerainty of the Seleucid empire, created by a lieutenant of Alexander the Great, Seleucos 1st Nikator.

In 190 B.C., during the war of Magnesia, the Romans conquered the Seleucid's Antichos III. Armenia took advantage of the victory to gain its complete independence. Its first kingdom was then founded with the advent of the Artaxiade dynasty and the accession to the throne of Ardashes I the Conqueror, a descendant of the Orontides.

In the same year, Strabo and Plutarch assert that the famous Carthaginian, Hannibal, who had taken refuge at the court of the Seleucids after being defeated by Rome, was in search of a new refuge after the battle of Magnesia. According to the Greek historians Hannibal found his refuge with the first king of Armenia who had just mounted his throne and was in search of a new capital to replace Armavir.

Hannibal approved the strategic and military importance of the new site, which was named Artaxata, the capital. A Roman general went so far as to call it the Carthaginia of Armenia!

In the following century Armenia experienced its era of greatest glory under the reign of Tigrane II who married a daughter of the famous king of the Pontus, Mithridates VI Eupator, immortalized by Racine.

At first reigning over a kingdom which included Armenia Major and Armenia Minor, Tigrane took advantage of a two-fold decline, the irremediable one of the Seleucids to the west and the temporary decline of the Parthians to the east, to build an immense empire stretching from the Mediterranean to the Caspian, and to take on the title of king of kings. In 66 B.C. he was conquered by Pompey who deprived him of his conquests but not of Armenia, which for a time became a Roman protectorate.

In relation to Armenian culture, Tigrane played an essential part, as René Grousset pointed out, in re-orienting Armenia towards the occident, as much by its Greek culture as its alliance with Rome.

In 62 A.D., the dynasty of the Arsacides (in Armenian, *Arshagouni*) mounted the throne of Armenia, inaugurating the second kingdom of Armenia over which Romans and Persians (Parthians at first, then Sassanids) continually quarrelled.

The very existence of this kingdom came to rest on a curious compromise between the two adversaries: a Parthian became king and a Roman crowned him. The Parthian was Tiridates I, brother of King Vagharshag of Persia, and the Roman was Nero who, in 66, made him come to Rome in order to crown him.

That was the time of the first Christianization of Armenia, evangelized by the apostles Bartholomew and Thaddeus, whose influence did not survive very long after their mission. However, the presence of these apostles in Armenia was enough for the Church of Armenia to later claim the title, "Apostolic."

At the end of the 3rd century, Armenia was once more, and this time entirely, evangelized by Saint Gregory the Illuminator, first primate of a long line of "Catholicoi" or heads of the Apostolic Church of Armenia. They chose to base their See at Echmiadzin, which in Armenian means "[the place where] the only begotten descended," and the Catholicoi reside there to this day.

Armenia adopted Christianity as state religion in 301 during the reign of King Tiridates III, twelve years before Constantine the Great instituted, by the Milan Edict, tolerance towards Christians of the Roman Empire. Armenians have always felt great pride in belonging to the world's first Christian state. Unfortunately, the zeal of the neophytes of the new faith destroyed all monuments bearing witness to the splendour of Hellenic paganism. Only the beautiful Greek temple of Erebouni (the ancient name of Yerevan) still exists. The new religion was nevertheless the inspiration for the construction of admirable churches which became forerunners of Romanesque Art.

In 387 the first partition of Armenia took place between Rome and Persia. Although but a shadow of their former selves, the Arsacides continued to reign over the Persian zone of Armenia, called Persarmenia.

The year 405 was that of a providential counter-attack, that of a touch of genius. To ward off the menace resulting from weakening royal power, and to give the new religion a truly national basis, it was necessary to establish a distinct Armenian national character. To that end, the Catholicos Sahak I gave his full support to a highly gifted monk, Mesrob Mashdots, to create a distinct Armenian alphabet. Mesrob's success led to the Armenian language replacing Greek and Syriac in church affairs and Persian in state administration.

Such an initiative gave rise to a symbol of sovereignty that gave Armenia a cultural individuality, a political force that held it together, inevitably unifying otherwise diverse interests and rivalries. In other words a distinct religion and alphabet gave the Armenian spirit an impregnable citadel....

It was about time! In 428 Persia overthrew the Arsacides and put an end to the second kingdom of Armenia. What a wonder! Just as political power was collapsing, Armenia's cultural power emerged and led to what is known as the golden age of Armenia, covering the whole of the 5th century, when writers, philosophers and poets cast the foundations of Armenian culture.

However, the enemy did not disarm. In 449 Sassanid Persia decided to impose Mazdaism (Zoroastrianism) on Christian Armenia, in other words, the worship of Zarathustra, distant predecessor of the French Cathars. Then, in 451, the famous battle of Avarayr took place, where the Armenian nobility, for once united, fought against the Persians with desperate zeal. The Armenians were defeated but so was Zarathustra. The Sassanids had to admit failure in the face of ferocious resistance put up by their adversaries. Prince Vartan Mamigonian, head of the Armenian army at that time, remains to this day the object of great veneration. Each year, for the last 1,500 years, the church celebrates his glorious memory during *Vartanants* or the patronymic feast of Prince Vartan.

The national resistance to the Sassanids prevented Armenian bishops from attending the ecumenical Council of Chalcedon summoned the same year by Rome in order to condemn monophysitism which continued to arouse sympathy in the Armenian Church (which had remained faithful to the Nicene Symbol of 325). From then on, the Armenian ecclesiastical community did not adhere to the conclusions of a council which they had missed for imperative reasons, whence the "schism," not to say "heresy" condemned by the supporters of the "two natures" of Christ, one divine and the other human. The Armenian "heresy" was opposed not only by Rome, but even more so by Byzantium, always eager to annex Armenia in order to dominate her church as much as her territory. Confining itself henceforth to positions considered to-day as "neo-chalcedonian," the Church of Armenia professed a doctrine according to which Jesus possessed only one nature within which the divine and the human were indissolubly linked.

This stand enhanced still further the prestige of the church in the eyes of the faithful, who saw in her the depository of a Christian identity that also had an intensely powerful national quality.

Another key factor of Armenian individuality lay in its linguistic identity as a distinct branch of Indo-European languages. In this context the great Indo-European expert Georges Dumézil taught that linguistics could give rise to the most unexpected historical discoveries. The author of *L'Idéologie tripartie des Indo-Européens* (The Tripartite Ideology of the Indo-Europeans) illustrated his opinion by citing the following fact, going back to the first century of the common era. The Roman and Chinese armies had advanced towards each other without meeting, separated by scarcely a hundred kilometres. On learning of its existence, the Chinese named Rome in their language by the strange form of "Fou-Loun," strange because the first syllable of the Chinese transcription, Fou, remained inexplicable contrary to the second, Loun, perfectly identifiable, since the Indo-European "r" becomes "l" in the language of Confucius, and therefore "Loun" was indeed Rome. But where did "Fou" come from? The wildest of theories were elaborated without giving a satisfactory explanation until the day that the eminent Sinologue Paul Pelliot realized that Rome in classical Armenian was called "He-Rom" (Rome in modern Armenian). There was the key to the enigma because the linguists knew that the Indo-European "h" corresponded to the Chinese "f." And it was thus that the scholarly world realized that China was aware of the existence of Rome through the intermediary of Armenia. Such are the miracles resulting from the comparative study of languages! One can therefore conclude that Armenia must have been the setting of a missed encounter between the two greatest empires of the ancient world, one to the east and the other to the west of Armenia Major.....

In 640 the Arabs invaded Armenia which preferred Muslim occupation to Byzantine intolerance, thus resulting in Syria and Egypt shifting to the Arab side; in other words, all of the so-called "monophysites" seized the first opportunity to abandon the very beautiful but very stubborn Byzantium.

The third kingdom of Armenia was founded in 885 when the Arabs allowed Prince Ashod Bagratid (in Armenian *Pakradouni*) to wear the royal crown. For nearly two centuries it was a glorious period, marked by the development of the architectural art of medieval Armenia and the genius of its great mystics. The capital of its kingdom, Ani, the "city of a thousand and one churches," carried this art to its climax. Further south, another kingdom, Vasbouragan, whose capital was near Van, on the shores of the lake of the same name, was equally prosperous under the rule of the Ardzrounis. If the town of Ani could boast the most monumental cathedral of Armenia, the island of Aghtamar in Lake Van prided itself with the admirable church of the Holy Cross whose simplicity and pureness almost made it, seven centuries ahead of its time, a pre-figuration of baroque art.

In 1045, Byzantium seized Ani and put an end to its kingdom. In this connection it is worth pointing out that the same dynasty of the Bagratids reigned in two separate branches over Armenia and neighbouring Georgia, except that the Bagratids of Armenia kept their throne only until the 11th century, whereas those of Georgia held theirs until the 18th century before becoming the Bagration Princes of Russia, amongst whom was the loser of Austerlitz...

Driving out Byzantium, the Seljuk Turks overran Ani in 1064, thus putting an end to two centuries of a civilization which had seemed more like a dream than reality.

A third of the Armenian population left the scene of desolation and founded a new state elsewhere. They set off under the guidance of the nobility, towards Cilicia, where, on the edge of the Mediterranean, they found a bountiful landscape, voluptuously green in the shadow of the Taurus Mountains. This paradise charmed the newcomers who thought they were living a new dream. There, in 1080, an Armenian Princedom or "Barony" was founded and placed under the authority of Prince Rupen, related, so they say, to the Bagratids. The Rupenids allied themselves to the French crusaders and, in the person of Prince Leon I (also called "The Magnificent"), put on the royal crown in 1198. This crown was offered by Pope Innocent III and the emperor Henry IV of Germany, son of Frederick Barbarossa. It was placed on the head of Leon I by the Bavarian Cardinal Conrad von Wittellbach who came to Cilicia for the occasion. Leon I reigned from 1198 to 1219 with Queen Sybille, who belonged to the royal house of the Lusignans of Cyprus, originally from Poitiers, and ancestors of the La Rochefoucaulds. The Byzantine Emperor Alexius III Angelus also sent a crown to Leon together with the warning, "Remember that Constantinople is neared than Rome."

On the occasion of the coronation, the Primate of Bavaria presided a delegation of bishops and theologians who had accompanied him and who, after crowning Leon I, explained what Rome expected of him in order to end the Armenian schism. Turning then to his own bishops standing near him, Leon I spoke briefly in Armenian so as not to be understood by his Catholic interlocutors, "Let us accept now, or pretend to accept, what they demand; later we ourselves can take a position more in conformity with our conscience." This was a clearly worded recognition that the king, though he could not do without the support of Rome, was also fully aware, perhaps better than anyone, that his clergy, and still more his people, could never accept the violation of the credo that made their church the indestructible pillar of Armenia.

Thus the fourth and last kingdom of Armenia, that of Cilicia, was very close to France as seen by the fifty or so marriages concluded between Franco-Armenian kings and lords. For a better assessment of the impact France had on Armenia in those days one need only refer to the fact that since that time Armenians use the term "baron" when greeting each other and which, in Armenian, has taken on the meaning of "Sir" or "Mister."

Leon I died in 1219 leaving his under-age daughter Zabel (Isabel) on the throne. She later married Prince Hetoum of Lampron (in Armenian Lampronatsi) known in history by the name of Hetoum I, king of Armenia and founder of the Hetoumid dynasty. This king, who reigned from 1226 to 1270, had the courageous idea of going to Karakoroum in order to seek an alliance with the Mongols against the Seljuks, a step whose initial success was, alas, short lived.

The Hetoumid dynasty died out in 1347. The crown then passed on to the Lusignans of Cyprus, whose last representative, Leon V, an Armenian through his mother, reigned only one year, from 1374 to 1375, when the Mameluks of Egypt and the Seljuks of Anatolia put an end to Armenian independence for the next six centuries. Some Armenian traitors delivered Leon V to the enemy. He was imprisoned in Cairo until the kings of France and Aragon paid a ransom for his liberation.

The last king of Armenia ended his days in Paris. Charles VI, whose madness had not yet manifested itself, put the Château of Saint Quen at his disposal. Leon V, who very generously, but in vain, sought to place himself as mediator between the kings of France and England, who were fighting the Hundred Years' War, died in 1393 and was buried alongside the kings of France. His tomb, which is still in the Royal Basilica of Saint Denis, is, for many Armenians, an important place of pilgrimage, and, until recently, was each year the object of a requiem mass celebrated according to the Armenian rite by the Bishop of Catholic Armenians of France.

Less than a century after the disappearance of its last king, Armenia fell under Ottoman domination, which meant new servitude but also new grandeur little recognised until now.

To conclude this brief summary let us once more quote the words of the eminent Armenophile, René Grousset, who wrote the following sublimely beautiful lines to which no one could be insensitive, "What remains is Armenian civilization itself, its cathedrals, its poets, its saints, its martyrs, its spirituality. And this indestructible spirituality is all Armenia."

2

The Ascent of the Amiras

The Ancestors

In eastern Turkey, on the banks of the Euphrates, is a town Armenians called Agn and the Turks Egin. Today it is called Kemaliye, named after Mustafa Kemal Ataturk.

Agn, which in Armenian signifies "eye," "spring" and "hope" comparable to the Spanish "el ojo de agua" (the water's eye), was founded at the end of the 11th century by a group of Nakharars, great feudal leaders of Medieval Armenia, who fled from the invasion of the Seljuk Turks.

Evidence of the founders of Agn was soon lost, but at the end of the 17th century Agn gave rise to a new aristocratic class, that of the Amiras, which legend links with the Nakharars. Far from deriding legendary narratives, in so much as they constitute the embellished expression of collective sagas invariably based on facts, we have no proof that the Amiras were the decendants of the Nakharars, but such an explanation should be mentioned.

With the exception of some families of authentic princely ancestry, such as the Dadians, who represented a minority, the credible ancestors of most Amiras appear in Agn between the end of the 14th and 16th centuries. They belonged to a class of gentry, akin to squires – half townsmen, half countrymen – who apparently had title to what they possessed and were free to move around.

They do not seem to have suffered from the endemic insecurity reigning in the eastern provinces of Ottoman Turkey, where, amongst other causes, were incursions of bandits who plundered everything in their way, carrying off the men and raping the women. Nor did they appear to have benefited from an autonomous status comparable to that enjoyed by Armenians in a few strongholds such as in the well known Zeitoun region, governed by four Armenian barons. All the men in Zeitoun were soldiers, a very rare sight among the Christians of the Empire. The saying goes that their wives bathed naked in the rivers, in full view of everyone, according to the testimony of an ecclesiastic who vouched for the modesty of the bathing and the splendour of the bathers!

Thus the Amiras came from families who for numerous generations belonged to a certain provincial elite but not, apparently, to the more prestigious one of the original founders of Agn. However, the next step was taken by a number of zealous acolytes wishing to discover a continuity between the ancient and the new aristocracy, linking the Nakharars and the Amiras. These zealots happily established accommodating filiation between the military nobles and financial magnates via genealogies adorned with titles rather than tangible proof.

The following facts dating from the 19th century are an anecdotal illustration of the notion of tradition and seem a good example of the reality of the times.

Let us quote the case with great panache of Ohannes Effendi Allahverdi, a famous banker and heir to the Amiras of the same name who, between 1850 and 1880, occupied high office as life-long vice-president of the Audit Office of the Ottoman Empire. This important person, a Catholic, was visited one day by two fathers from the Mekhitarist monastery of Venice who said to him:

"Excellency, you no doubt know that your family descends from the Gamsaragan Princes. Will you authorize us to collect the evidence for this kinship?"

"What will you base your researches on fathers?" asked Ohannes Effendi.

"Ah, Excellency," replied the fathers, "We will base it on oral tradition which alone exists in the Orient."

"In that case," answered Ohannes Effendi, "you can abandon your project, I am content as I am."

Half a century earlier Megerdich Amira Djezahirli, who will often be mentioned in these pages, could have spoken similarly. Knowing by hearsay that he was the descendant of Princes and even Kings, he decided to carry out some research and asked two priests, who did not know each other, to draw up his family tree. He received two different genealogies![*]

The debate concerning the Amiras' ancestors is still open and one has to accept that the history of Agn, the modest melting pot of a brilliant elite,

---

* Born at Sivas in 1670, the Abbot Mekhitar (in English the consolator) was persecuted for his Catholic faith and fled from Turkey. He took refuge first in the Pelloponese and then, when Morea was invaded by the Ottomans, he fled to Venice. In 1712 he founded, with the Pope's support, the Mekhitarist Congregation, who were given full possession of the Venetian island of Saint Lazzaro. From the 18th century Armenia owed those monks, who accomplished remarkable works of research and publication, a true renaissance of national literature. Mekhitar died in Venice in 1749 after publishing a grammar and dictionary of the Armenian language, as well as an Armenian edition of the Bible. Today the Mekhitarists possess an important collection of Armenian incunabula decorated with medieval illuminations of exceptional beauty.

remains shrouded in mystery. Why did almost all the Amiras originate in Agn? Why were the Agntsi* more or less the only people to occupy a unique sort of power? These questions remain largely unanswered, at the very point where reality and fiction, history and legend meet. The society of Agn constitutes a historical enigma, comparable to a state of grace arising from a mixture of tradition, culture and way of life conferring an exceptional influence on its members.

When the Osmanlis,† who practised the highest degree of the refinements of oriental *savoir-vivre* inherited from the pomp of Byzantium, saw these young men of good standing arrive at Constantinople, they were soon charmed by their distinction, the elegance of their manners, and the subtlety of their intelligence.

One can but wonder how the Amiras adapted themselves to Ottoman domination. From the moment that, for reasons still to be elucidated, they considered themselves capable of leaving their mark on Turkish power, they submitted the latter to their formidable desire for power which they used with the greatest care and determination.

Though they did not consider themselves Turks, they did not feel strangers in a Turkey whose people they knew well and whose language they spoke as fluently as their own. Hostile to all ideas of retreat, exile and still more rebellion, not wishing to confine themselves to their province, nor to seek fortune elsewhere, and certainly not dreaming of an impossible independence, the Amiras thought that only the capital of the Empire could satisfy their quest for power. They therefore established the masterminds of Armenia on the shores of the Bosphorus, the masterminds that nourished the dual ambition of assuming control over the imperial administration and Armenian national affairs. Their power spread quickly but had to remain, of course, hidden, because of the only barrier they never wished to cross: conversion to Islam. Of the one hundred or so Amiras recorded in the 18th and 19th centuries, we only know of one who abjured his faith, and that was for a lack of choice. Apostasy would have been considered a flaw, and a stain, both of which were shameful.

Nowadays Armenians sometimes qualify other Armenians who served the Turkish Empire as "traitors". If such a judgement is conceivable after the genocide of 1915, it is truly anachronistic for the earlier period. Indeed,

* Agntsi (*Arm.*): Inhabitant of Agn.

† That is to say the Ottoman court.

"betrayal" was not serving the Empire, but serving Islam. The Amiras were undoubtedly too attached to the Armenian national church to embrace the religion of Mohammed, even if conversion would have made most of them Grand-Viziers!

Obviously, and with no scruples, the Amiras favoured the Turkish card, but an autonomous card, and therein lay their distinction and interest of action: A distinction in relation to their predecessors who didn't hesitate to convert to Islam, and a difference with regard to Turks whose religion they did not profess, even if this led to their exclusion from honours reserved for the believers in the "true faith."

The refusal to convert and the privileges linked with the denial of their faith constituted, in a way, the "exoneration" of the Amiras who thus by-passed the barrier they did not wish to cross, while acceding to honours and eminent functions. Why did these aristocrats wait until the end of the 17th century to quit the banks of the Euphrates for the shores of the Bosphorus? Their decision perhaps aimed at stemming the decline of the Armenian Patriarchate of Constantinople.

The Patriarchate

Intimately linked to the lives of the Amiras, the Patriarchate of Constantinople was the pride of Ottoman Armenians. It symbolised, within the framework of the Empire, both the national identity and the Christian belonging of Armenia.

To fully understand the importance of these links, it is necessary to go back to the conquests of the Byzantine Empire and the capture of Constantinople by the Turks in 1453. The fall of Constantinople was also the beginning of the Patriarchate of Constantinople, the result of an initiative, not of the Armenian Church, but in reality, the Ottoman Empire. We do not know precisely to which sultan this initiative should be attributed: Mehmed II (1432–1481), Selim I (1467–1520), or Suleiman the Magnificent (1494–1566). On the other hand, we know for certain that this Patriarchate was a Turkish creation which, for centuries, was to determine the evolution of Ottoman Armenia.

According to tradition, now questioned, the creation of the Patriarchate is attributed to the conqueror Mehmed II. A political genius, as much as a military one, Mehmed II sought to conciliate the people he conquered. And if he did not seek to convert them to Islam, he certainly used tolerance as a calculated move: because Muslims were exempted from paying a tribute tax, it was necessary to have a sufficient number of infidels to support the Treasury.

The political status granted to the minorities undoubtedly carried the mark of the genius of Mehmed II. By "political" status, one should understand political-religious status. Indeed, instead of Byzantium, the conqueror founded a theocratic Islamic empire, an Ottoman version of the Byzantine Caesaro-papist one, within which Mehmed introduced theocratic vassals (Greek, Armenian, Jewish) headed by the dominant theocracy, whose vassals were less territorially than religiously defined. The fundamental structures of the Ottoman Empire were organised around these axes.

Thus, within the framework of the Turkish, Islamic and sovereign nation, other nations were also recognized, based on faith but not on Islam. Each of these minorities was to be administered by its leading ecclesiastical head having the rank of an Ottoman "minister" and destined to be, in the name of each respective nation, the official interlocutor with the Sultan as the self-proclaimed Caliph of all Muslims. This latter status applied not only in Turkey but the world after the Ottoman conquest of Egypt in 1517 by Selim I, to whom the last Mameluk Sultan of Cairo had surrendered his title of "Successor of the Prophet."

The merging of religion and national identity had such an impact that the national criterion was overshadowed by the religious one and Christians and Jews were considered as forming the two key denominational elements (other than the ruling Muslim one). Any of their members abandoning their faith, as occurred frequently in the 15th and 16th centuries, lost their national identity and became Turks, according to the principle that all Turks were Muslims and all Muslims were Turks. Thus it was that in the 17th century Muslim Albania gave Turkey a remarkable dynasty of reforming Grand-Viziers, the Köprülüs.

Concerning their non-Islamic minorities, the Osmanlis, up to the end of the 19th century, had a marked preference for Armenians. By Osmanlis one means the sovereigns of the empire rather than the practitioners of Islam, the former being much more tolerant that the latter.

Mehmed II was the first to set the example by multiplying advances to Armenians, by inviting them massively to Constantinople, and using their services more and more each day.

Pursuing the logic of his policy to an extreme, Mehmed II took a sensational decision in 1461 when he created the Armenian Patriarchate of Constantinople. By this unprecedented gesture, which conferred the same rank and prerogatives on the new institution as the thousand-year old ecumenical Patriarchate, he raised, psychologically and symbolically, Armenia to the same status as imperial Byzantium.

The homage paid to Armenia went above all to its church. Having always personified the existence of a "nation," the Armenian church had managed to preserve a religious autonomy which compensated for the loss of Armenian political independence. In this regard one can be struck by the convergence between the conception of Mehmed II and the vocation of a self-governing church, considered, via the nation-religion link, as a natural substitute for national sovereignty. Such an explanation accounts for the manner in which Armenians were more or less prepared to accept Muslim domination which, paradoxically, advantaged their church.

The Sultan thereby accomplished a highly seductive act, an example of Muslim tolerance. He carried out his plans admirably and thus penetrated into the driving force of the Armenian soul... One might almost say that the beneficiaries of his policy were ensnared by his advances.

The skilful Turk had carefully calculated his course of action regarding Armenia. And his calculations were far from being unintelligent. By seeking to be agreeable to Armenians he followed three goal: he ensured the cooperation of Armenians; he used Armenians to counter-balance Greek influence; and he removed all temptation for Armenians to turn to hostile Persia where the Catholicos, the Supreme head of the Armenian church, resided at Echmiadzin.*

By establishing a Patriarch of Constantinople, the Ottoman rulers showed a creative tolerance that was favourably received by the Armenian nation. In addition, this same volition profited the Jewish minority for whom a Chief Rabbi was established and recognized, whereas the Ecumenical Patriarch of the Greek community was simply maintained. These three religious leading figures, hailed as *Millet Bashis*,† were

* Armenia at the time was divided between Turkey to the west and Persia to the east. At the start of the 16th century the major part of Armenia was in the Ottoman Empire with Erzeroum as the main town, while Persia kept Echmiadzin until the Russian conquest in 1828.

† Millet Bashi (*Ott. Tur.*): Head of nation or community.

responsible for the administration, under the authority of the Sultan, of all non-Muslim minorities of the Empire. If the non-Hellenic orthodox faithful (Serbs, Bulgarians, Romanians...) were "spiritually" attached to the "Greek nation" (*Rum millet* in Turkish) and administered by the Ecumenical Patriarch, the non-orthodox faithful, the "non-Chalcedonians" according to modern terminology (Copts, Ethiopians, Assyrians, Chaldeans, Jacobites, Syrians...) were, as the Ottoman conquests progressed, attached to the "Armenian nation" (*Ermeni millet*), thus enlarging the new Patriarch's field of action. On the other hand, the Chief Rabbi was confined only to the Jewish sphere.

It will be noted that the Catholics were not mentioned in this list which only included Oriental Christians, whether Orthodox or not. This omission was not accidental. As a theocratic power, the Empire did not tolerate its subjects to be subservient to a pontiff external to the Ottoman world. The Roman religion could only be practised by strangers, the very ones whom Suleiman the Magnificent placed under the protection of François I by granting him capitulatory rights in 1653. France thought that this protection covered all Christians of the Empire, though it only concerned Latin Christians. Amongst the Armenians there were some Amiras, and not those of least importance, who professed the Latin faith but were obliged, by Ottoman law, to pledge allegiance to the Patriarch of Constantinople, which gave rise to incredible situations and all sorts of conflicts.

Before ending this passage concerning the creation of the Armenian Patriarchate of Constantinople – in fact the Patriarchate of Turkish Armenia – one must mention an episode indicative of oriental compromises which were, perhaps, more imagined than real. But we know that the interpretation given to events by popular belief sometimes counts more than the events themselves, and such beliefs express more faithfully the deep tendencies of an era.

On the eve of his conquest of Byzantium, Mehmed II contacted an Armenian prelate whose diocese was the one nearest to the future capital of the Empire. Hovagim was bishop of Brussa (Bursa) and since 1326 this town had been the Ottoman capital, that is, prior to Andrianople (Edirne) and Constantinople. The sultan said to the prelate, "I am off to conquer Byzantium. If you pray for me and my victory, if you bless me and if I succeed, I will make you Patriarch and patrician with jurisdiction over the whole Empire." Why did the Turk attach such importance to the blessings of an infidel? The bishop didn't have a second's hesitation. Bowing before Mehmed II and with a steady hand he made the sign of the cross on the standard of the Muslim prince, all the while murmuring, "The patrician is well worth a sacrifice."

This collusion between a religious person and a man of Islam, at the expense of a dying Christian empire, though very dismaying, is nonetheless revealing of a particular state of mind. Byzantium had always inspired in Armenia a mixture of fascination and revolt. For a very long time – and far longer than Rome – Byzantium fought to subjugate the Armenian Church. Paradoxically, Muslim enemies, first Arabs, then Turks, proved more tolerant than Christian brothers. The parallel is striking, at this level, between the creation of the Armenian Patriarchate of Constantinople after the Turkish conquest of Constantinople, and eight centuries earlier, the establishment of the Armenian Patriarchate of Jerusalem upon the Arab conquest of that city. In each case Byzantium paid the price of its doctrinal intransigence and played into the hands of its Muslim adversaries: Armenia preferred to submit to the enemies of Christianity, who allowed her to practice her religion freely, than to the great Christian powers who persisted in persecuting her. The independence of the church took precedence over that of the State.

Illustrating this state of mind are the words of the Byzantine Great Admiral Notaras, who declared, when the Empire was collapsing, that he preferred to see the turban of Mohammed (Mehmed) II at Saint Sophia than the hat of a pontifical legate, indicating the extent of the implacable hatreds opposing the Christians of different confession.

As for Armenia, it was undoubtedly more dangerous for her to deliver herself to Muslim domination than to the intrusions of Christian Byzantium. But in 1453 it was too late, Byzantium was dying and Rome was far off; the crusades were a thing of the past, the disastrous campaign of Nicopolis having been the last convulsion half a century earlier.

Be that as it may, the Armenian Patriarchate of Constantinople had become a reality, arising from a pact concluded between a political giant and a cynical bishop, between the Crescent and the Cross, which, in spite of all the barriers raised between Islam and Christianity, was to favour incredible moments of interpenetration as long as the Ottoman Empire lasted.

But, from the second half of the 17th century, the decadence of the Patriarchate set in, mediocre men succeeded each other as its leaders, and even secular men got themselves nominated Patriarchs. It became an urgent matter to restore the dignity of the institution, and it was then that a vanguard of the future Amiras went to Constantinople and took control over the Patriarchate which is still situated near the Bosphorus at Kum-Kapu.

Assuming Power

Within a few years the new arrivals had imposed their authority. It was in fact just a helping hand, but it sufficed to place at the head of the Patriarchate, in 1715, the greatest primate in the history of Ottoman Armenia. It concerned a simple vartabed,* only 37 years old, but radiant with intelligence as well as humanity. His name was Ohannes Golod. The new Amiras, most notably Seghpos Amira Yerevanents and Yaghoub Amira Ohannessian, who count among the most illustrious of the Agntsi, escorted the newly elected primate to Sultan Ahmed III who at the time resided at Adrianople and whose approval was necessary for his investiture. Nominated by an Imperial Firman,† Patriarch Golod returned to the capital, where his restorative reign lasted no less than 26 years (1715–1741).

Golod Patriarch distinguished himself from his predecessors who had been incapable and mediocre men who had discredited the Patriarchate during the previous decades. He had the great honour of being consecrated bishop at Constantinople by the Catholicos, the supreme head of the Armenian church. The seat of the Catholicos was mostly under Persian rule but was conquered and remained in the Ottoman Empire for a dozen years (1724–1736).

The Ottomans greeted the Patriarchs with a reverential formula, *"Patrik Effendi"* ("Monseigneur the Patriarch"), although the title *effendi* was reserved by right for members of the Imperial family and the dignitaries of Islam. Granting such a title to the two Christian primates – Greek and Armenian – was, on the part of the Muslim authorities, rendering to the Christian "heads of nations" a homage that was worth noting.

The part played by the Amiras within the Armenian *millet* was of major importance, though it should be pointed out that all of their authority came, above all, from the credit granted to them by the Sublime Porte‡ and

* Vartabed (*Arm.*): Celibate theological doctor, future bishop.

† Firman (*Ott. Tur.*): Edict, decree.

the pressure subsequently exerted on Turkish administrative and political bodies.

What did the Amiras do to be accepted by the Ottomans and to satisfy their thirst for power? The road to honours was barred to Christians who could not be admitted to major state functions. The only sphere accessible was that of finance, the power of money, in so far as Islam forbade Muslims to trade in the precious metal and above all to grant loans with interest.

The Amiras thus gained, because of Islamic laws, the power to control Islam at the expense of its civil servants. Their stroke of genius was that they realized the immense use they could make of the venality of the Empire's expenses, which allowed them to defy Islamic interdictions and circumvent its taboos.

Most of the Pashas had to buy their offices. The Amiras encouraged the Sublime Porte to generalize the venality system and to increase the sums necessary for Muslims to acquire state offices, while they themselves offered to lend the necessary sums to such candidates. The state and the Pashas were thus under obligation to the Amiras, who had themselves become the guarantors of the Pashas, guaranteeing not only their functions but still more their submissiveness, failing which they withdrew their protection and the Pashas lost their office, if not their lives. This is how the Amiras, Armenians and Christians, terrified their Ottoman and Muslim masters. On querying the spirit of such a system, one will note that it gives an astonishing lesson of political balance, between conquerors and conquered, between Muslim guarantees and Christian guarantors. It can also be seen that from this set-up, both unforeseen and original, emerges a morality of exceptional wisdom that is characteristic of the Orient.

Between the end of the 17th and the middle of the 19th centuries, the Amiras formed a very powerful bloc composed of around one hundred magnates, mostly Agntsis. Previously, influential Armenians were not lacking in the imperial capital, but they came from other towns in Asia Minor and exerted their power individually, as, for instance, Abro Chelebi[*] who, through his birth and his power, is considered as the precursor of the Amiras. He was a descendant of the Bargratides[†] and was himself the

‡ Sublime Porte: Name given, in a wider sense, to the administration of the Ottoman Empire.

* Chelebi (*Ott. Tur.*): Prince.

† See chapter 1.

ancestor of statesmen who governed Ottoman Egypt in the 19th century: Boghos Bey, Nubar Pasha, Dikran Pasha.*

On the contrary, the Amiras found themselves, as already mentioned, at the head of a real *Agntsi* network and, during almost two centuries, masterminded and dictated their law on the Empire through Turkish Pashas. This term of an "*Agntsi* network" is most appropriate. Not only did the Amiras, despite their differences, constitute a perfectly identified social class, but their collaborators, from their main assistants down to the humblest of their employees were also recruited in Agn. Such employees were duly sent and picked up by trusted men as they stepped off boats at Constantinople and were then escorted to the khans† of their masters.

Nubar Pasha (1825–1899)

A more precise idea of the part played by these magnates is given by the testimonies of foreign observers, all the more interesting because they did not always like Armenians. Thus, David Urquhart, an English diplomat accredited to Constantinople in the 1830s, published a book in 1833 entitled *Turkey and its Resources,* which is one of the best referenced works concerning the history of the Amiras.

After describing the venality of the offices of state as "the hidden resource which sets into motion all the administrative machinery of Turkey," Urquhart continued as follows:

> The Armenians have been and still are the richest and most commercial people of the empire; by their wealth they are the surest guarantees to the Porte... The sultan views their prosperity with no unfriendly eye, as their wealth, like that of the pashas, is not squandered by extravagant habits, or expended in rebellious

* See chapter five section on the Karakehia.

† Khan (*Ott. Tur.*): Inn, office.

> enterprises, but remains carefully hoarded in their strong-boxes till some pretence, or some necessity, brings it into the miri [treasury]. Considerable capital being required for carrying on this branch of business, the number of the sarafs [brokers, bankers] is, I believe, under eighty, nearly the number of the pashas; and as, by their refusal to become guarantee, they can reduce any Turkish governor to the condition of a private individual, they, in fact, farm out the provinces at their pleasure and for their profit; they have even of late carried their authority so far, that no banker will consent to become the saraf of a pasha — raised, as I may say, to that rank by one of their body, without a note of hand from his former banker, declaring that all his demands have been satisfied... ...[T]he Armenians have, from their wealth, connection, and party feeling, sufficient influence, even to contribute to the nomination of the grand vizir himself.*

Twenty years later, in 1853, Ubicini repeated these observations in his *Letters on Turkey.*

The Pashas, as we said, quite often risked losing their life. An Amira could also lose his. It was not frequent but was in the nature of things. For instance, in the event of a Pasha being condemned to capital punishment by the Sultan's order, the same punishment could also be applied to the Amira who had granted him his caution. This is what in 1821 led Kasbar Amira Cherazian to the gallows, guilty of having guaranteed the well known Pasha of Jannina, Ali of Tebeen, who had been guilty of rebelling against the Sultan. In this case Pasha and Amira were united in death after being united through gold.

Envy and denunciation added their blows since Turks were confronted by around a hundred Amiras whose personal fortune could attain several million pounds sterling at that time.

Faithful to their temperament, the Turks, except those guaranteed by the Amiras, displayed a superb indifference towards them in an indolent manner so specific to their character. Then, as time went by, the nonchalance changed into jealousy and one day into fury: then death was demanded, re-establishing, in a certain manner, an equilibrium characteristic of Turkey. In his history of the Ottoman Empire published in

---

* Urquhart, *Turkey and its Resources,* London, 1833, pp. 107-109.

Paris in 1817, Salaberry thus evokes, "The Ottoman is in turn furious and docile, each step marked by crime and repentance."

This "restoration of equilibrium" could take a long time to come about even if envy and calumny flourished all over Constantinople. But one never knew when or where they would chose their target and swoop down on their prey. The relative immunity of the Amiras was due to their financial power, as well as the rank of their protectors in the upper Turkish hierarchy, even if the latter were always liable to an eventual disgrace.

What is the meaning of the title Amira which entered the Armenian language in the 7th century when the Arabs conquered Armenia? It is the Armenian version of the Arabic *Amir, emir,* just as the word "amiral" (admiral) is the Gallicised version of the Arabic *Amir al Bahr* (Prince of the Sea). During one thousand years, from the 7th to the 17th century, the title *amira* designated, in the Armenian language, the Muslim princes, before the title was bestowed on Armenian dignitaries by Ottoman Sultans.

Anahide Ter Minassian summed up well when she wrote:

> ...the sultans rewarded some very rich Armenian civil servants with the title of Amira. At the end of the 18th century, there were about a hundred Amira families some of which... were real dynasties. By their number, the privileges acquired, the hereditary transmission of their titles and offices, the Amiras constituted a class perceived and described, until the middle of the 19th century, as a new aristocracy.*

Traditionally, the word Amira was inserted, in the Turkish manner, between the forename and the surname. Often, moreover, the forename sufficed. During the period with which we are concerned, this title was only given to Armenians who were raised to a rank which gave them five prerogatives very rarely granted to non-Muslims:

* exemption from the tribute to which every infidel was bound

* authorization to wear the imperial *toughra* (i.e. the coat-of-arms of the reigning Sultan) embossed on their *kalpaks* (large spherical-shaped headgear)

* the right, greatly sought after, to wear noble furs (ermine, sable, lynx)

* the right, only reserved to Muslims, to ride horses,

* the privilege – exorbitant and eminently Islamic – to wear a beard, while infidels were only allowed to wear a moustache, with which the

* Anahide Ter Minassian, *Histoire des Armeniens*, Prival, Toulouse, 1982.

Amiras generally contented themselves as a precaution, even though they were imperially authorized to let their chests be covered by silvery glints of a luxurious beard. They knew that, for a beard to be really permissible, it could only be Turkish and Muslim… If Byzantine Constantinople was still hesitant concerning the sex of angels and whether women had souls, for Ottoman Constantinople there was no possible doubt that faith and law were male to the extent of being bearded!

Hereditary nobility not being accepted in the Ottoman Empire, titles and privileges were renewed each generation, except for that of *Bey*, bestowed on the sons of Pashas and other important personalities. In the 18th century, the Europeans in Constantinople, and notably the diplomats, greeted the Amiras with the respectful title of "Banker Prince." As for Armenians, they generally gave them the title of *Ishkhan* (Prince) in Armenian.

Other than the banker princes there was another class of Amiras, less numerous but more brilliant. It was composed, for lack of a more adequate term, of what one could call "senior civil servants" belonging to four dynasties: the Duz, who gave the Empire a succession of senior administrators of the Imperial Mint which controlled the striking of the small gold marvels that were Turkish pounds; the Balian, who, during six generations as imperial architects, gave Turkey a galaxy of builders who built not only palaces adorning the Bosphorus but also some of the most beautiful mosques of Istanbul – the jewels of Islam – conceived by Christian genius; the Manasse, who gave no less than eight generations of portrait painters and miniaturists to a court whose Sultans, due to Islamic prohibition, preferred to be portrayed by Armenian hands; and finally, the Dadian, descendants of the Ardzrouni princes and perhaps the most illustrious of all, who, during a century, bore the prestigious title of *Baroutdji Bashi,* meaning the Grand Master of the Gunpowder, in other words, of armaments. It was, moreover, in their factories that the best arms of the Empire were made. Therein resides one of the major paradoxes of an Empire where Christians couldn't be soldiers, but a Christian family was granted the means of arming the soldiers of the same Empire….

Let us add that the accountants of the Duz were all Armenians, as were the stone masons of the Balians, and the artisans of the Dadians; the account books of the senior administrators of the Mint were kept in Armenian, and similarly, the plans and sketches drawn by the imperial architects were accompanied by commentaries written in Armenian. It seems that the records of the Baroutdji Bashi regarding the production and maintenance of their arms were also written in their national language.

This convergence of monopolies resulted in not only a formidable banking lever but also the striking of money, artistic creation, and the fire power of the Ottoman Empire being concentrated in Armenian hands. Without playing on words, one could say that these Amiras had the upper-hand on the gold, the arts, and the arms of Imperial Turkey which, under their influence, experienced an incomparable development. It is, perhaps, no exaggeration to say that, during the 150 years of their power, the Amiras had been the secret masters of the Ottoman world.

Control and Protection of Armenia

As discrete manipulators of the upper Ottoman hierarchy, the Amiras remained, quite openly, the rulers of Armenia. The power that they held at the court of Constantinople made them the unmistakable masters of their "nation" which, in the 18th century, was around two million souls. They were indeed their despots, but enlightened despots, not because of a philosophy of "Enlightenment" which had spread throughout Europe, but the impression of being the guardians of a cultural and religious tradition.

With regard to the Armenian nation, the political and economical influence of the Amiras manifested itself through three reins of power over which they had complete mastery: control of the Patriarchs of Constantinople, the guarantee of provincial governors, and the levying of taxes.

Officially the Amiras were the counsellors of the Patriarchs who presided over the National Assembly which included the aristocracy, clergy, and delegates of the middle-classes and artisans. In the event of a crisis, nearly a thousand representatives could gather at the Patriarchate. In fact, the Amiras exercised their financial and political power by making and unmaking Patriarchs as they pleased to the point of turning them into instruments of their own will. The first to benefit from this situation were the Turks, in so far as each accession of a Patriarch gave rise to the payment of a substantial sum to the Treasury, which could be called the patriarchal contribution; of course the Amiras clubbed together to pay the sum. Considering the dissensions which, alas, existed between the Amiras, it sometimes happened that several patriarchal candidates were sponsored simultaneously by different Amiras. It was then to the highest bidder that the Sublime Porte gave its preference. What difference was there, then, between these new abuses and the period of decline that the Amiras were supposed to have averted? If they placed on the patriarchal throne men devoted their cause, they also did not dare clash with influential prelates such as Ohannes Golod who combined political firmness with episcopal charisma. Besides, is it not the eternal secret of the Oriental church to have always been the plaything of Caesar and to have also known how to mock him?

As for the provincial governors, the fact that they were "guaranteed" their position by the Amiras gave the latter indirect control of Armenia and the possibility of administering, through intermediaries, the Armenian inhabited provinces of the Empire. In the event of unwanted exactions, they could always undermine governors by withdrawing their backing.

There remained the levying of taxes which was also a considerable source of power. That was the most controversial sphere of action of the Amiras, accused by some of having enriched themselves at the expense of the taxpayers. Although inevitable abuses were committed, the Amiras were entrusted by the Sublime Porte not to squeeze money out of the population but to prevent the Pashas from doing so. Their mission was indeed to control the collection of the tribute by the governors, by ensuring fair and correct receipts, but not to actually levy the taxes themselves. They were not the collectors but the guarantors. The morality and interest of this form of power resided in the fact that the Ottoman government trusted Armenians more than Turks to supervise fiscal policy. In the event of the provincial governors failing in their duty by embezzling the receipts, the Amiras were obliged to repay, from their own money, any tax usurped by the tax collector. The financial sphere was thus, from every point of view, as risky as it was profitable to the private property of the Amiras.

In the eyes of their contemporaries the piety of the Amiras was their main title to glory. It is in no way astonishing that Armenians recognised in their church the necessary conditions for their survival and glorified the art of such survival. The Armenian chronicles of the time frequently evoke only the piety and not the full part played by the personalities cited. Let us take the example of Yaghoub Amira (1672–1752) who held the office, considerable for a Christian at that time, of *Bazirguian Bashi*, senior administrator of the economic life of the Empire. If sources scarcely mention his attributes, they are not, on the other hand, lacking in details concerning a pilgrimage this Amira made to Jerusalem at the age of 75 in 1751, or the donations he made on this occasion to the Monastery of Saint James, so dear to Armenians. Nothing is lacking: sacerdotal vestments, the details of their embroidery, the weight of the candelabras, the size of the candles, not forgetting the particular, a chandelier in solid silver weighing, so it is said, not less than 74kg! For all that, was Heaven grateful to the Amira who was hung on the gallows the following year? Truly unfathomable are the ways of Providence....

In the sphere of religious fervour, the absolute criterion rested on the building of churches. Each Amira had to build his own, which had to be more beautiful than that of the others, and an Amira existed in the eyes of posterity only through the sanctuary of which he was the builder and the donor.

If historians lack for sources of information, the faithful, for their part, were not lacking in temples. In this respect the Amiras not only carried out pious deeds but also useful works, giving those gathering in their churches the chance to rediscover what Armenians possessed as most authentic: a very beautiful liturgy, majestic as much by its rites as by its admirably intense chants, particularly in the interpretation, semi-feminine, semi-masculine, of the poignant solos of *"Der Voghormya."*[*]

The lords of Ottoman Armenia built not only churches but also schools, printing works, hospitals, orphanages. Judging by the importance of their pious foundations, their action was precious to the Nation for safeguarding their identity.

One of the most spectacular gestures accomplished in this context was that made in 1831 by Artin Amira Kazaz, thanks to whom we venture into the world of *miracles of the Orient*. The recently completed steeple of the church in Haskeoy[†] was one day accused of covering, by its height and the peal of its bell, the shrill voice of the muezzin of a nearby mosque. The Turks demanded and obtained permission for the demolition of the steeple, much to the displeasure of the Armenian community. In order to save the situation, the Armenian community asked Kazaz Amira, to whom immense credit was given and had incomparable "savoir faire," to intervene. One day

* Der Voghormya (*Arm.*): "Miserere mei, Deus", "Lord Have Mercy on Me."

† "Village of Purity" in Turkish, Haskeoy was a small town near the Golden Horn and harboured some of the greatest Amira families.

Kazaz entered the imperial carriage and sat beside Sultan Mahmoud II whose love of Armenia has become proverbial. Just as the carriage and horse approached the Sweet Waters of Kiathane, Kazaz looked very ostentatiously straight ahead. "What are you looking at, Artin?" asked the sovereign. "Oh Padishah," answered Kazaz, thus resuming in one admirable word the Islamic-Christian complicity of the time, "I am looking at the church of Haskeoy where Jesus and his holy mother Mary pray for the precious days of your Highness. Alas, this church is the object if an unjust punishment from some people who have ordered the demolition of its steeple on the pretext that it smothered the voice of a muezzin."

"I'll look into the matter" decided the Sultan, who ordered the carriage to halt and looked speechless at the mutilation which put him to shame. At the end of his silent contemplation, Mahmoud II ordered not only that the steeple be rebuilt, but that its height be doubled. Thus it is that, on the injunction of the Caliph, Commander of the Faithful, and first servant of Allah, the steeple of the little church of Haskeoy took off towards the sky surpassing all the steeples in Constantinople and competed even with the most slender minarets.

This example, resembling a legend, illustrates beautifully the manner in which Amiras knew how to plead the cause of their church, in other words, of their Nation. It illustrates once again the way in which the Amiras – like the rest of their co-religionists – manoeuvred in a bicephalous world. Being in contact yet not blending into a truly hierarchical entity, there coexisted on one side the Empire (Turkish) and on the other the Nation (Armenian).

Armenians, Greeks and Jews

The progressive elimination of Greek and Jewish "competition" brought, one may say, the power of the Amiras to its zenith in the 19th century.

These minorities, alas, did not get on well together, nor did the Amiras. With regard to the rest of the world, the Armenians evidently did not benefit either from the prestige of the Greek spirit, or the Jewish way of thinking. Without questioning their intellectual value, they themselves did not claim to be champions of any universal philosophy or any major influence. That is, no doubt, the underlying reason for the Turks' preference, to whom they brought their talent without overshadowing them.

Admittedly, it would have been better for these minorities to have united their efforts to present, in the face of the Empire, a common front whose force might have changed the face of the world. But how can one add up three singular traditions, each three thousand years old?

Let us reflect on this subject in relation to Armenian-Greek history and Armenian-Jewish relations.

The Byzantine Empire had for a long time persecuted the Church of Armenia, contrary to Rome, which showed more understanding to the kingdom of Cilicia. On the other hand, Byzantium presented the most fascinating period of Armenian glory outside Armenia.

Do we know how many emperors Armenia gave Byzantium? The famous dynasty called Macedonian was Armenian. The great emperors such as Nicephorus Phocas, Romanos Lakapenos, John Tzimiskes had Armenian ancestry. This is a source of pride of which all Armenians should be fully aware.

The Greeks today, as it happens, are very honest and recognize the imperial role of Armenians, whereas Turks totally reject all they owe to Armenia.

At the time of the Amiras, Armeno-Greek rivalry created less havoc than one might have feared because there was a certain distribution of tasks between the two minorities. The Greeks had a monopoly of the dragomanate,* whereby they controlled the foreign policy of the Empire. The Hospodars of Walachia and Moldavia, who were Turkish vassals, were recruited from the Greek aristocracy, the union of the two regions later giving birth to Romania. The Greeks were also involved with banking, but in a subsidiary way. A persistent hostility, on the other hand, pitted Armenians and Greeks against each other over the Monastery of Saint James of Jerusalem, coveted by the Greeks but confirmed as the possession of Armenians in 1517 by Sultan Selim 1st who wanted to please Armenians when he conquered the Holy Places.

It has been seen that the Amiras, except for the Senior Civil Servants, concentrated their action on the banking monopoly; there they were in direct competition with Jews. Less ancient than the Armeno-Greek relationship, the Armeno-Jewish contacts dated back to the end of the 15th century, when Jews driven out of Spain found refuge in the Ottoman Empire which welcomed them. They very quickly took possession of the banking instrument in which, for two hundred years, Armenians got the

* From the word *dragoman* which designates the official interpreters at Constantinople and in all the Levant.

worst of it. Progressively, the Amiras reversed the situation by depriving the Jewish bankers of their prerogatives, one after another. A decisive blow was struck on the Jews when the management of the Imperial Mint was taken out of their hands in 1758 and entrusted to the Armenian Mikael Duz. Finally, in 1826, the massacre of the Janissaries, ordered by Mahmoud II, put an end to their important function as bankers to this group of the elite. The elimination of the Janissaries coincided with the disgrace of the Greeks, following the Hellenic war of independence, so that the Amiras became the undisputed masters of the land for the last fifty years of their power.

The Profession of Faith of the Church of Armenia

For greater clarity and an understanding of the endless religious quarrels, it is helpful to discuss some theology and avoid any ambiguities.

Armenians are frequently confounded with the Orthodox, either by mistake or convenience. Yet they are not Orthodox in the sense that for Orthodoxy, as for Catholicism, Christ possesses two natures, one divine, the other human, by virtue of which the Churches of Rome and Constantinople are called "diophysites" (two natures), whereas that of Armenia is considered to be "monophysite" (one nature).

In history, monophysitism normally appears as a doctrine which attributes the Christ only a divine nature endowed with just a human appearance. Hence its condemnation by the Council of Chalcedon in 451. The Armenian Church was, in consequence, and for a long time, accused of a schism, even heresy. But the so-called monophysite profession of the Armenian Church is not heretical. It is related to no "appearance." It professes, it is true, that Christ possesses only one nature, but within this nature the divine and the human are indissolubly bound. The human is placed on the same level as the divine, which is the essential, and Armenians take care not to follow the example of the great heresiarchs of monophystism, nor that of the Eutyches who professed that in the person of Jesus the divine took precedence over the human, nor of Nestorius who taught the contrary. In other words, the Church of Armenia has always abided by the "unique nature" recognized by the first Christian Council of Nicea in 325.

These subtleties may seem vain. Nevertheless, the Church of Armenia sees in her profession of faith the need of a unique specificity whose profound reasons, in the beginning, could only have been of a political nature.

Overall, there are more similarities between the Churches of Armenia and Constantinople than between those of Armenia and Rome. Armenians and the Orthodox have the common appurtenance of the Oriental clergy, the marriage of parish priests (but not of prelates), the same restrictive interpretation given to the origin of the Holy Sprit who, according to them, proceeds only from the Father, whereas for Rome, he proceeds also from the Son, as expressed by the famous controversy of "*filioque*" or the Procession of the Holy Sprit.

However, despite the misunderstandings now corrected by ecumenism, the Armenian dialogue has been easier with Rome than with Byzantium, in spite of the reservations attached to the primacy of the Pope.

Paradoxically, it is within the framework of the Turkish Empire that the Catholic Church showed intolerance to Armenians and pushed the Patriarch of Constantinople to side with the Ottomans. One tenth of the Armenian population of the Empire was of Roman Catholic confession. We think that Catholic Armenians joined the warmth of the Orient with the rigour of the Occident. An undeniable courage was required to profess Catholicism in an Empire which, as already seen, did not accept that some of its subjects pledged allegiance to the pontiff outside the Ottoman world. These Armenians could not have been unaware of the transgression of this rule. Let us recall in this context that the Patriarch of Armenia was accountable to the Porte for the submissiveness of all Armenians.

From then on, the Catholics had to be extremely prudent, but this was not the case with Latin missionaries. The latter sought, by every possible means, to "Latinise" Armenian Catholics, who had been permitted by Rome to keep their rites and their language, although they had no place of worship of their own. To compensate for this insufficiency, the Catholic Amiras installed secret chapels in the most remote parts of their palaces, where they secretly received the faithful. But the Roman clergy did not give up. Whenever the "Latinizing" pressure became too great, word reached the porte and led to the re-enaction of an unchanging scenario: the Grand-Vizier convened the Patriarch and asked him for an explanation; the prelate admitted that a handful of Catholics escaped his authority; some people were then imprisoned, but after a few months, upon the payment of a huge sum, they were freed. The bugbear of Catholicism thus served to fill the coffers of the Treasury. Sometimes a few heads rolled, but rarely.

It is evident that the victims of these reprisals came from the faithful, guilty of allegiance to Rome, and not from the Latin clergy, who were protected by the intangible immunities of which France was the leading guarantor.

3

The Arbitrations of the Ambassador of France

In 1731 a fire devastated the Armenian church of Saint Gregory the Illuminator in Constantinople, the only one situated in the "Europeanized" quarter of Galata. It was much loved by Armenians. Its reconstruction (1732–1733), financed by Seghpos Amira, aroused a great outburst of faith. "Both sides" of the population took part in the rebuilding, signifying that the Armenian-Catholics brought their contribution to the *Apostolics*.* This "collusion" displeased the Latin bishop and his preachers who forbade their Armenian flock to frequent churches other than the Latin ones. Furious, the Grand-Vizier Ali Pasha Hekimzade admonished Patriarch Golod, reproaching his lack of firmness, and informed him of his will to stiffen his position concerning the "adepts from abroad." The patriarch, who was on very good terms with his Catholic compatriots, insisted of warning them of the danger, but his interlocutors ignored his warning. The Turkish government made some arrests and placed guards in front of Latin churches in order to ban access to Armenians, thus showing that the defenders of Armenian Catholics were not unknown to the authorities.

After such a snub, the Latin bishop requested the intervention of the Ambassador of France in 1734. The representative of Louis XV to the court of Constantinople was, at that time, the Marquis Louis-Sauveur de Villeneuve, who represented the Ottoman politics of France.

To start with, the Ambassador considered it appropriate to strike a decisive blow. In agreement with the Ambassador of Germany, he protested to the Sublime Porte against "the attack on the honour of his country."

In the face of such an offensive, the Ottoman government released the prisoners and removed its soldiers. The Patriarch immediately profited by this truce to resume his charm offensive and to follow his life-long dream: an understanding between Catholics and Apostolics, in favour of which he had already agreed with Catholics and cancelled in 1727 the anathema that had been cast by the Church of Armenia against the Council of Chalcedon. While still remaining wholly faithful to his own church, Golod Patriarch knew the importance of the Church of Rome, whose order and discipline he admired, and he sought to turn relations to his advantage.

* See Malakia Ormanian, *Azkabadoum*, Constantinople, 1913.

For the time being, he interceded with the Ambassador and the Catholic church to obtain a certain reciprocity. Thus, after opening the doors of Latin churches to Armenian Catholics, the Patriarch asked that Armenian Catholics should be allowed to enter Armenian churches. In reply, the Patriarch's interlocutors again asked for the famous anathema to be lifted, especially as some over-zealous Apostolic priests still referred to it. A *modus vivendi* was established which reduced the causes of friction without removing them entirely.

The next scare came from the Apostolics, amongst whom were not only over-zealous priests. One of the most important, Shirin Khalfa Amira, who held the post of imperial architect and considered the Patriarch as too favourable to the Catholics, simply bribed the Grand-Vizier Mehmed Pasha Esseid to send for Golod Patriarch and order him to better supervise his *millet* – and to hand over those who were "unruly." In fact, corruption and denunciation were constant occurrences in the Ottoman empire. Taking the warning seriously, the Patriarch convened the Catholic Amiras and told them of his fears, which were shared by his listeners, who returned to Armenian churches to the great displeasure of the Latin clergy.

It was then, in 1735, that Ambassador de Villeneuve took, in total secrecy, a very courageous initiative. He had the idea of building an Armenian Catholic church which would be independent of the Latin clergy, who, he thought, extorted too much money out of the Armenian flock. The new church would be placed under the dual authority of Rome and the Porte, and the faithful would, with their own priests, celebrate their services as they wished, while paying their dues not to the Latins but the Patriarchate.

By achieving such a feat of conciliating obedience to the Vatican with Ottoman subjection – without breaking off relationships with the Patriarchate which remained the legal façade of Armenians – this project showed the exceptional broad-mindedness of a visionary diplomat who, a century before his time, foreshadowed the status finally granted – due to French pressure – to Armenian Catholics of the Empire. (Once recognized, Catholic Armenians were to be released from an allegiance to the Patriarchate and possess their own Patriarch). But what seemed logical in the 19th century was not necessarily so in the 18th century. Be that as it may, the Catholic Amiras supported the ambassador's plan enthusiastically. They collected and handed him the funds for the construction of the sanctuary whose purpose was still kept secret.

Of course the secret was discovered and the Latins and Ottomans united against the project, the former being concerned about the loss of their advantages and the latter because of the obedience to foreigners such changes implied. A war having broken out between Turkey and Persia, Villeneuve took this as a pretext to put off, until the end of hostilities, the realization of a plan which, finally, was abandoned… for a hundred years.

Armeno-Greek squabbles soon followed the Armeno-Latin quarrels which were also unexpectedly arbitrated by the Marquis of Villeneuve.

We know that the Holy Places were, and still are, divided between the Latin, Greek and Armenian clergy. At the start of the 18th century, as a result of bad management, negligence and all sorts of abuse, the Patriarchate of Jerusalem was riddled with debts almost to the point of being confiscated. Such a development would have delighted the Greeks. In 1715 a saintly man, Mgr Krikor (Gregory) of Shirvan, bishop of Moush, a colleague of the Patriarch of Constantinople Golod, and as enlightened as him, was approached by the latter to save the Armenian Holy Places. Mgr. Krikor, on becoming Patriarch of Jerusalem, was much appalled by the situation he discovered. While appealing to the Amiras and his nation for donations, he set himself up as "*prisoner of the debts*" and had an iron collar welded around his neck, like collars used for chaining prisoners, and he vowed not to remove it until all the debts of the Patriarchate were entirely cleared. Without flinching, he endured this trial for eight years (1718–1726), at the end of which, Armenian Jerusalem had regained its ancient splendour. This is why Patriarch Krikor is remembered as the "*Bearer of Chains*" (in Armenian *Shkhtayagir,* in Turkish *Zindjirli.*)

In 1727, the Patriarch of Constantinople obtained permission from the Sublime Porte, through the intervention of Seghpos Amira, to restore the "Armenian quarter of Jerusalem," which was more than an implicit recognition of the rights of Armenia. Such authorization was requested from the Turkish government for all architectural works, building or repairs. But, in the face of Greek manoeuvres, Mgr. Golod wanted still more and profited from the good mood of the Grand-Vizier, Ali Pasha Hekimzade. In 1734 Golod obtained, through the meditation of Seghpos Amira, a *firman* renewing in due form the "ancient imperial writs" recognizing the Armenian presence in Jerusalem.

The Greeks were greatly discontented with this *firman* and swore to have it revoked. They took advantage of the nomination of a new Grand-Vizier,

Ismail Pasha Gurdji, to corrupt him in their favour. This Grand-Vizier remained in power for only six weeks, but for Armenians these were six weeks of nightmare. Seghpos Amira, guilty of negotiating the renewal of the *firman,* was thrown into prison and a courier was hastily sent to Jerusalem to recover the said firman and render it void. Rumour had it that Seghpos Amira was to be beheaded. This would perhaps have been the end of Armenian Jerusalem, but for a providential quarrel breaking out between the chief of the eunuchs and the Grand-Vizier, resulting in the destitution and deportation of the latter. The Grand-Vizierate was then entrusted to Mehmed Pasha Esseid, who was favourable to Armenians and immediately freed Seghpos Amira.

This frequent change of Grand-Viziers calls for a commentary. The powers of these Prime Ministers of the Empire were as far-reaching as they were short-lived. They were exercised by men who could be subjected not only to the charms of Christian tempters who handled money as a weapon, but also to the whims of an imperial arbitrator, himself under the orders of a clique of courtiers both fickle and corruptible. This state of affairs probably did not help to counteract the decline of the Empire; it was a far cry from the authority and competence of Grand-Vizier Koprulu in the previous century.

In the Jerusalem affair, Armenians benefited from unforeseen support. The claims to exclusive ownership of the Holy Places put forward by the Greeks also constituted a menace to the Latins of Jerusalem who, from then on, sided with Armenians. This rapprochement, which took place at the beginning of 1736, was immediately followed up in Constantinople where dissensions between Catholic and Apostolic Armenians were ironed out with the combined help of the Marquis of Villeneuve and Patriarch Golod. The Patriarch also invited the "Bearer of Chains," hallowed with sanctity and respect with a letter signed by twelve prelates and twenty-three Amiras requesting his presence and helping hand, despite his great age and fragile health.

Mgr Krikor left Jerusalem on May 6th 1736 but arrived at Constantinople only on July 28th owing to difficulties during the journey and his health problems. In the capital he was greeted by the Patriarch with, writes the chronicler, "as much emotion as humility." The Marquis de Villeneuve sent two Latin clergymen to welcome him. Mgr Krikor replied,

"Ill, I come to seek recovery, and unhappy, I am in search of consolation," adding that he wanted the Ambassador's help.

Whilst the Greeks remained in expectation, those wishing to harm the reconciliation between Catholic and Apostolic Armenians whispered to Villeneuve that the Patriarch of Jerusalem, when saying Mass in a church in Samatia, had made blasphemous remarks concerning the Latin liturgy. But the Ambassador, "a wise man experienced in religious quarrels," gave no credit to this gossip. On the contrary, wishing to impress public opinion in view of the "entente," he gave a great reception dinner at the French embassy in honour of Armenians on the evening of February 3rd 1737 to which he invited the Patriarchs of Jerusalem and Constantinople as well as a certain number of Amiras.

No such event had ever been seen within living memory. Until then, only the Catholic Amiras had been able to pride themselves on being invited to the French Embassy.

M. de Villeneuve placed the "Bearer of Chains" to his right and Patriarch Golod to his left. The prelates profited by the occasion to request the lifting of the ban placed on Armenian Catholics to attend Armenian churches and the Ambassador asked them to see to that concerning the anathema. At the end of dinner, M. de Villeneuve offered a magnificent fob-watch to each of the two Patriarchs who took leave in an atmosphere of mutual satisfaction.

At the beginning of March 1737, the Ambassador arrived in great pomp at the church of Saint Gregory the Illuminator in Galata, accompanied by his family, his collaborators, and his leading compatriots. This procession aimed at encouraging Catholics not to abandon Armenian churches. On April 8th he went to the Latin Church of St. Benedict, also in Galata, where he wished to see the Armenian Good Friday procession, which he knew was quite impressive. He requested the procession to make a detour via St. Benedict where he honoured it by setting all the bells ringing. This was enough to hear extremists on both sides murmuring, "The Ambassador is becoming Armenian and the Patriarch is becoming Roman."

In 1737 there was a change of the Catholicos at Echmiadzin. A bishop called Kutur, known to be an intriguer, represented at that time the See of Echmiadzin in the capital and hoped to keep himself in that position. However, he thought that he had been removed through the intervention of Mgr Golod and using the suppression of the anathema against the Council of Chalcedon as a pretext, he stirred up extremist Apostolics to lynch Mgr. Golod.

Ambassador de Villeneuve did not fail to complain to the Sublime Porte. To add weight to his protestation and with his taste for the spectacular, he made an audacious mixture between the Council of Chalcedon and France, saying that the angry crowd had cast an anathema against the sovereign. Very embarrassed by this offense towards "the greatest King of Christianity," the Grand-Vizier dispatched a high-ranking official to Mgr. Golod, accompanied by forty soldiers, asking him to forbid any anathema against the King of France, to which the Patriarch replied that it was a long time since his Church had excommunicated anyone. The Turks were bewildered by all this. But the inveterate partisans of the anathema nonetheless continued to refer to it. Six of them were imprisoned on the spot. Bishop Kutur took fright and hurriedly sought refuge in Persia.

M. de Villeneuve multiplied the arbitrations. He asked the Patriarch to show him the text authenticating the rights of Armenians on Jerusalem so that he could intercede with the Sultan and establish an order confirming those rights. He was also assigned by Louis XV to act as mediator in the war opposing the Ottoman Empire against Russia and Austria, after which the Ambassador, whose good offices lasted no less than a year, went to the theatre of operations in Belgrade.

Peace, obtained to the advantage of the Ottoman Empire, was concluded in Belgrade on September 18th 1739 under the patronage of M. de Villeneuve whose prestige became still greater and had an unhoped-for effect. Aware of his irresistible influence, the Greeks abandoned the unequal struggle and, renouncing their claims, made peace with Armenians. Even more amazing, this peace was signed at the French Embassy! The agreement was drawn up in Italian, presented as the "international language of the time," and bore the signatures and seals of the four Patriarchs (Greek and Armenian of Constantinople and Jerusalem) and of the Amiras and Greek princes. It explicitly stipulated the return to the status quo, each of the two parties remaining in control of their possessions, and the Greeks recognizing that the Copt, Ethiopian and Assyrian clergy were placed under the authority of the Armenian Patriarch.

Three months before the conclusion of this agreement, Mgr Golod had sent a letter to Cardinal Fleury, via the Ambassador, setting out the facts to the Prime Minister of Louis XV. The answer expressed a marked sympathy towards Armenians, assuring them of French protections without raising any problems of a confessional nature.

In 1740, Sultan Mahmoud I, through the intervention of de Villeneuve, delivered the *Hat-i-Sherif** to the Patriarch, permanently confirming all the rights of Armenians.

Did the Greeks appeal to the French Ambassador requesting him to obtain a comparable decree in their favour? Did de Villeneuve comply with their request? History does not tell us. We only know that finally the "three nations" – Latin, Greek and Armenian – received, under the care of the brilliant diplomat, the imperial guarantee of equality of rights and the inalienability of their possessions.

The "Bearer of Chains" then returned to Jerusalem where he ended his days in great veneration. Patriarch Golod, whose vocation as a reformer and a conciliator was unfailing, passed away on February 13th 1741 after twenty-six years in office. His death was followed closely by the departure of the Marquis de Villeneuve, who left an everlasting impression in Constantinople. Yet his work and name are all but forgotten today!

Finally, Seghpos Amira, eminent benefactor to the Armenian nation and senior administrator of the economic life of the Empire, was condemned to death at the same time as the Grand-Vizier Mustapha Pasha, whose guarantor he had been. Both were beheaded in 1755, the Amira being, according to a scenario already described, considered to be the accomplice of a government leader fallen into disgrace. Seghpos Amira, then aged 75, knew of the same fate that befell his contemporary and counterpart, the octogenarian Yaghoub Amira, who was executed three years earlier for obscure reasons, edifying examples of the unpredictable ways of Ottoman justice which could wait a long time before brutally striking down powerful and often innocent men.

The grandson of Seghpos Amira, Jean de Serpos, converted to Catholicism and having become a Venetian in the second half of the 18th century, was successively made a Polish Marquis, a Roman nobleman, and a patrician of Venice, where he led a distinguished life under the name of Giovanni di Serpos.

---

* Decree of Sherif.

Map of the Bosphorus circa 1850

4

The Universe of the Amiras' Influence and Decline

Romances, Delights, and Tears

In the second half of the 18th century, around 1775, a delegation of European diplomats who were in search of wives called on the Patriarch of Armenia to explain to him that the conditions of life in Turkey condemned members of the western Embassies in Constantinople to celibacy because no woman could accompany them without being forced to live the life of a recluse.

These diplomats pointed out that, with the exception of the Ambassador of France, whose presence on the shores of the Bosphorus amounted, so to speak, to a taboo, the members of the Embassies were obliged, surprising as it may seem, to live in a hotel, in what was called a *khan.* In this case it was Elchi Khan situated opposite Vezir Khan of Tavouk Bazar, an important centre of the capital.

Need one recall that all female presence was banned from such places? It would have sufficed for one western woman dressed *à la franca* to appear in the street to inevitably invite the abuses of passers-by and the barking of dogs.

An obvious incompatibility existed between the importance Turkey attached to the friendship of France and the insults addressed to the French by the Turkish lower classes. The Turkish authorities did not dare to take severe action against these insults, so tenacious and deeply-ingrained was the hostility towards everything that was not *à la turca.*

Having come to the conclusion, remarkably objective for the time, that Western and Armenian churches were very close to each other, these distinguished visitors requested permission to seek wives among the daughters of the Banker Princes, on the understanding that they would submit themselves to all confessional requirements. Did these negotiators think that they were back in the time of the Crusades, when many noble Francs married beautiful Armenian women whose eyes were as black as their blood was blue? During three hundred years the Crusaders had the merit of promoting the western epic of an Armenia that the Ottoman conquest later on plunged into the deep Orient.

The request formulated by these westerners could not have come at a more ill-timed moment. At that time the Patriarch of Armenia was the austere and intransigent Zakaria II, an implacable conservative, unsympathetic to the drawbacks of a lack of spouses and opposed to conclude alliances, particularly matrimonial ones, with a world considered to be the exact opposite of his. Consequently, the proposition of the plenipotentiaries irritated him as much as it surprised him. He nonetheless replied to his eminent interlocutors that the request would be examined with the greatest attention by the council of Amiras and prelates which he himself presided.

Patriarch and Amiras held an emergency meeting. They could, after all, have been sensitive to the fact that the petitioners preferred Armenians to Greeks, who were better known in Europe. But this preference seemed to have eluded entirely the then masters of Armenia, who saw in the projected marriages a risk of alienation rather than a mark of honour. They vetoed what seemed to them above all the danger of "being Gallicised," a spectre that suggested, at best, the snares of westernization and, at the worst, a pact with the devil.

Their descendants in the following century, some sixty years later, abandoned this outlook. But, for the time being, Patriarch Zakaria, happy to have averted the peril, summoned the European diplomats to notify them of the refusal by Armenia to give their daughters to Europe. Having learnt from this set-back, the western negotiators turned towards the Greeks and saw the ecumenical Patriarch complying to their request with an unsurprising benevolence, the only condition laid down, and accepted, being the observance of the Orthodox rites.

The contrast between the character of these two people, between the Greek availability and the Armenian rigidity is illustrated by this distressing example. It is likely that on the Greek side they were not sorry to get the better of Armenians who, in this affair, had made great fools of themselves by reacting as slaves of the Turkish mentality and by paying the price of an extraordinary missed opportunity.

The diplomatic delegation had emphasized that western women could only live in Turkey as "recluses." However, oriental women, as were Armenians, also lived cloistered in their homes, where, apart from their husbands, they were not allowed to see men other than their fathers or their brothers. They could not go out unless well accompanied and veiled from head to toe. There, too, customs copied the Turkish model. The Ottoman world was a particularly male chauvinist one.

Given this context, what do we know of the love-life of the Amiras? Practically nothing has come to light concerning their gallantry, be it their passions, their fantasies, or their escapades. They married very young, or rather, they were married off very young. When such arranged marriages were not happy ones, what did the men do if they were sensitive to the appeals of the flesh? Owing to the extreme compartmentalization of a world that refused well-born women all contact, the flighty husbands had no choice but the facility of beautiful courtesans or the accessibility of winsome peasant girls whom they brought from their Anatolian estates and, after tasting their charms, gave them away in marriage – after richly endowing them – to one or other of their young associates.

To men the mediocrity of the courtesans, to women the gloom of the gynaeceum. The only exception to this rule known so far is found in the evidence left by the Dutch painter Jean-Baptiste Van Moor who, in 1725, depicted *Armenian Society Playing Cards*. This scene is totally incompatible with the canons of the time. It can concern but a tiny minority, in other words, the uppermost class of Armenian society, probably Catholic, which gives the impression of scoffing at the most institutionalized taboos.

This painting by Van Moor, kept at the Rijksmuseum of Amsterdam, is reproduced in the admirable *Pages d'art Arménien* published in Paris in 1940 by the very elegant Armenag Bey Sakiz, son of the last Armenian to have occupied the post of Finance Minister of the Ottoman Empire. These *pages* are a "modèle du genre" bringing to life again, and with much charm, the elegant Armenian life of 18th and 19th century Constantinople.

Considered by some people as a precursor of Guardi, Jean-Baptiste Van Moor had been the portrait painter of five French Ambassadors who, from the Marquis de Ferriol to the Marquis de Villeneuve, successively represented their country, notably to Sultan Ahmet III. This enlightened Sultan reigned from 1703 to 1730 and was the father of the "Era of the Tulips," (in Turkish *Lâle Devri*), the name given to one of the periodic attempts to westernize the empire in order to wrench it from its demons. Incredibly, pashas would be seen wearing Louis XV costumes and great ladies exchanging their veils for crowns of bright red tulips.[*]

The *Armenian Society Playing Cards* is named by others *Around the Tendour* after the brazier placed under the card table where charcoal is burning slowly. The heat given off is maintained by a very thick tablecloth covering the table and the knees. This enveloping way of fighting off the cold is very effective.

Armenag Bey writes, "We must suppose that playing games was at that time a favourite pastime and sufficiently characteristic of Armenian society," the painting by Van Moor "constituting a document of undeniable authenticity."

Nevertheless, this painting merits a closer look. The people highlighted in this scene are strange. It seems very improbable that at the start of the18th century Armenian society tolerated women, freed of the constraint of the *yashmak** and wearing low-cut dresses, to sit at card tables in the company of male players whose fur collars attested to their rank.

The sight given by this *tendour* us bewildering. There seem to be quite a number of women players – at least six – lit by a single lamp in the Chiaroscuro tradition of the Dutch school, all young and pretty, all simpering behind their cards and looking steadfastly at their partners. One could attribute the liberties of this picture to the "Era of the Tulips."

But it must be admitted yet again that the testimony of Van Moor is limited to a minute social class representing the most progressive members, the most westernized, an Armeno-Catholic world playing willingly with fire. Besides, Armenag Bey himself professed the Roman religion.

In fact, it is not so much the card game in this composition that draws attention as a series of attitudes incompatible with the canons of the time: the completely anachronistic banter between the two sexes, unless the painting is representing a strictly "intimate" scene as suggested by Armenag Bey.

Before closing this chapter, let us quote an example of thwarted loves situated around 1830.

Hagop Amira Tinguir (a great Catholic name) had a devastatingly beautiful daughter called Veronica. The Tinguir's neighbour was the Greek Prince Constantine Ghika, son of Gregory VIII, Hospodar of Wallachia. It

---

* A pre-eminently Turkish flower, the tulip decorates the sumptuous earthenware of the Iznik School (Nicaea) whose artists were often Armenians. Deriving its name from the Turkish *tolipend* (that is to say turban), it appears to have been cultivated initially in Turkey. To please Holland, whose infatuation with this flower he knew, Sultan Ahmet III sent a profusion of the most beautiful varieties in the form of bulbs, thus contributing to the spectacular development of this flower in the land of the polders.

* Veil making the face invisible.

is said that Constantine and Veronica fell in love with each other from their respective balconies. The prince requested the young girl's hand, which, despite the difference of religion, was granted him by her mother and brothers (with the exception of one brother, Artin Amira), and they agreed to the ceremony being celebrated according to the Orthodox rite. The marriage took place unknown to the recalcitrant brother and the young couple "went away" but where did they go at a time when honeymoons were still unknown? The newly married couple simply covered the short distance to settle down at Constantine's house. Artin Amira remained inflexible and became very angry. He decided to move heaven and earth to break up this marriage, unless the husband converted to Catholicism, which was out of the question since the Hospodars were obliged to profess the same religion as their subjects. The Amira went as far as to mention this affair to the Sultan, asking him to pronounce the separation. He declared that the Prince had abducted his young girl who, he said, being twelve years old was "neither nubile nor sensible," even though she had all her wits about her and was at least twenty years old. The Sultan, accustomed to the intrigues of the harem, the practice of polygamy, and the facility to accept the breaking of marriage bonds – albeit Christian – gave an imperial order to lock up the young woman in her father's house and send the young man to his paternal abode. The couple put up a desperate resistance to these instructions. Constantine was taken by force to Wallachia and Veronica was exiled to Angora (Ankara) "to recover her senses."

There was also a comparable story of the daughter of a priest, an "apostolic" Armenian, who in 1827 disregarded her parents' refusal and married an Englishman. This situation led to great public unrest in an Armenian population which was closed to the outer world. The subsequent disturbances took on such a dimension that the Patriarch had the young woman kidnapped under the Englishman's nose and shut her up in a hospital from which she was freed by the British Ambassador who gave her back to her husband. But this example of a happy ending was very rare in those days.

Court Painters and Other Men Skilled in the Arts

We have just evoked a Dutch painter and his unusual work throwing some light on Armenian society of the day. This society had also given rise to a dynasty of painters, equally unusual, as much by the duration of their office as by the nature of their works. We say "offices" because they were Court painters through eight generations. The members of this dynasty, bearing the name Manasse, exerted their talent from the start of the 18th century up to the end of the 19th.

Although the links between the artists and the financial world may be tenuous, the Manasses have their place in this book dedicated to the Amiras. Not only were they of the same religion as their contemporaries, but they exerted a comparable influence during the two centuries of their existence. Let it be noted in passing that such a duration is a record in a world opposed, in principle, to the notion of heredity.

We have already mentioned to what extent the Amiras manipulated the Porte through financial transactions forbidden to Muslims. As a result, the Pashas were less dependent on the commandments of Islam than those of Banker Princes.

The painters, in their way, also manipulated the Turks. Since Muslims were not allowed by their faith to reproduce a human face and still less that of a Sultan, they secretly entrusted Christians to paint their portraits, which they hid in the depths of their palaces. No doubt these liberties with regard to the Koran troubled the Turkish conscience, but they also show the extent to which the same Turks had a solid sense of emancipation, or perhaps, scepticism.

As for the artists themselves, they were not lacking in talent, of which they made excellent use in the creation of miniatures and portraits of Ottoman monarchs. The Manasse very quickly sounded the death-knell of the cultural hegemony of Muslim Persia under Mongol influence at the court of Constantinople by being the best representatives of the French, and sometimes the Italian, schools. Strangely enough, they combined artistic and diplomatic careers in the service of Turkey by appearing in Paris, Vienna or Milan as First Secretaries, Consul Generals, etc...

At the end of the 18th century the most illustrious, Raphael Manasse, nicknamed "The Raphael of the Orient" by the Chevalier d'Ohsson (Ignatius Tossounian) in his *Tableau Général de l'Empire Ottoman*,* took the opportunity to mention the difficulties encountered by artists in the Empire. "How, indeed," he writes, "could they progress in the sublime art

---

* *Tableau Général de l'Empire Ottoman* was the first monumental history of Turkey in French. It was published in Paris at the end of the 18th century by the Armenian d'Ohsson who was related to the great Armeno-Catholic family, the Nafilyans. He was a dragoman, then Swedish Ambassador to the Sublime Porte.

amidst a nation which pays no attention to it, where one encounters no sort of model at all, where even Christians have no taste for pictures, nor are they in the habit of having their portraits painted, and where, finally, painters, either Greek or Armenian, have no choice in exerting their talents but to paint the images of saints decorating churches, chapels and private houses?"

The Duz Princes were an exception to this rule; Armenian Catholics, they all had their portraits painted, each indeed more austere than the last. The portrait of Sarkis Chelebi Duz,* painted at the beginning of the 19th century by the French artist Louis Dupré, left a somewhat affected impression of him but interesting by the expression, attitude and costume adorned with a magnificent sable fur collar, a mark of his high rank.

Sarkis Chelebi Duz (1777–1819) painting by Louis Dupré.

Let us also mention, again by this same French painter, a very beautiful portrait of the Armenian Pascal Artine Chelebi, who, as Crown Jeweller, was one of the artists on friendly terms with the Sultans. In 1819, Dupré made a remarkably subtle portrait of him as an Oriental man in all his splendour, squatting on a couch in the Turkish manner, wearing a turban and holding in his hand an elegant *chibouk.*† The neck and the rest of the pastel blue cloak are edged with a long sable fur collar, confirming the rank of the sitter.

Around 1830, Sultan Mahmoud II, who was unconcerned about any form of sectarianism, had a medal engraved with his effigy from the portrait painted by Zenop Manasse, which he hung on a chain, making it the highest distinction of the Empire, the Order of *Tasvir-i-Humayoun.*

---

* Today in Venice (on the island of San Lazzaro) at the Monastery of the Mekhitarist Fathers.

† A sort of long pipe, more than 1m long, not to be confused with the *narguileh* (hookah).

Mahmoud II was even more daring in defying the taboos of Islam. He decorated public offices with a life-size portrait of himself by the same Zenop.

In 1850, another member of this family of artists, Rupen Manasse, painted a portrait of Sultana Fatma, the eldest daughter of Abdul-Medjid. The miniature is all the more worthy of mention since it portrays a Muslim princess.

At the end of the 19th century, Sultan Abdul-Hamid II, known to be a fanatical Muslim, greatly appreciated the talent of Joseph Manasse (1835–1916), the last representative of the dynasty. Abdul-Hamid asked him to paint the German Empress, wife of William II, who was visiting Constantinople in 1899.

Finally, let us point out that Armenia gave Ottoman Turkey outstanding craftsmen who, without being artists, were nonetheless "men skilled in the arts."

Let us, for instance, mention the discovery made at the end of the 18th century at Kouzgoundjouk, on the Asian shore of the Bophorus, of a method of painting faces on fine muslin, called *yazma* in Turkish. Production was concentrated in Scutari and the fashion spread throughout the Empire. We know that it was the work of an Armenian who had no link with the Court and was probably more of a craftsman than an artist. His name is unknown.

Amongst all these "men skilled in the arts" we shall end by evoking the memory of those 19th century Armenians of merit and high rank, almost a dozen of whom received the title of Pasha. In the preceding century, the famous doctor Boghos Andonian-Shashian (1744–1815) was the first Armenian of Constantinople to study abroad. From 1762 to 1769 he was in Italy and was able to pursue serious medical studies. On his return to Turkey he became First Imperial Doctor and treated Sultans Abdul-Hamid I and Selim III. He was also the appointed doctor of the Amiras of his time. His son, Doctor Manuel Shashian (1775–1855) was the personal physician of Sultans Mahmoud II and Abdul-Medjid. The latter made him *Commander of the Iftihar* and personally decorated him with the insignia.

The Amiras' Way of Life

In her *Souvenirs de famille et d'Orient*, published in Paris in 1916, Marianne Damad – whose mother was a Duz – faithfully depicted the rules of *savoir-vivre* to which Armenian society complied. "The education given to us in our ancient families," she writes, "was very refined. We were trained to be polite and amiable, and we were taught the art of never saying something which might offend others. On the contrary, we were always to seek words which others would find agreeable. The ceremonial, in all circumstances of life, was the rule, erudite, complicated, strict." She concluded with a detail whose elegance must be underlined, "Yes, decidedly, this flower of Oriental politeness was a pretty thing. I can see my father bowing to the servant who helped him remove his overcoat or galoshes in the hall of a friend's house. My father's bow to this servant had a courtesy as great, perhaps even greater, than if he had addressed a celebrity."

A wise saying gave Armenians cautious advice which was not always followed. In Armenian, this saying had a special flavour: "*Kloukht shad veru mi haner vor chi gdren yev shad mi dzrir vor chi gokhen,*" which can be translated: "Do not lift your head too much lest it be cut off and do not lower it too much lest it be trampled on."

The Amiras observed this warning by, for instance, having the exterior of their houses whitewashed, thinking they would thus not attract attention. If by the external appearance of their life-style they rarely transgressed the rule of voluntary self-effacement and apparent asceticism, it was quite different in the intimacy of their homes where, out of sight, the prudent Orient became the opulent Orient.

During the cold season, the Amiras lived in the old town, taking refuge in the shadow of a screen of steep and winding streets that hid the thresholds of the vast winter abodes, the *konaks.* The enigmatic life of their owners was visible even in the conception of these residences which, hiding their treasure as a fur-lined coat hides its fur, sheltered an interior of marble behind a plaster frontage.

These precautions knew a kind of respite when the fine days of summer appeared and the mask of austerity melted in the heat as the Amiras changed houses with the season. To the tormented landscape succeeded the sovereign harmony of the Bosphorus. On the shores of the famous straits it was but a shimmering of greenery and azure. The luxuriance of nature submerged the luxury of the people. Summer saw the reopening of the palaces, the *yalis,* real jewels built of old wood and bathed, on the edge of the waves, by the fascinating encounter of water and light. Everything, people as much as things, contributed to make this site and its dwellings an exceptional place, "a diamond set between two emeralds," according to the famous Ottoman expression.

One is entitled to be surprised by the contrast between the winter precautions and the recklessness of summer. Some people will plead the use, very widespread in Turkey, of wood as a building material, even if it is artistically sculptured wood, whereas it was inconceivable to exhibit publicly the marble of the Christian *konaks*. But, despite the marble being covered in whitewash, it was known to the Pashas who were received into these houses. These secrets were thus open secrets, unless the aim was to fool the Turkish lower classes whose reactions could sometimes have been dreadful. But who could have been fooled by the size of the *konaks,* huge to the point of containing almost fifty servants who – a significant detail – walked always barefooted to avoid any noise that might disturb their masters?

How were these palaces furnished? Simply, in the Turkish manner, with sofas, low tables and carpets. Sophistication was visible on the walls where magnificent Chinese plates were hung, and on the tables where Dresden china and Bohemian crystal were set out, some spherical, like the delightful *kerse*s,* others oblong with a handle like the *ashourelik*s. These objects consisted traditionally of a saucer, a container with a lid, the latter always decorated with a rose. The *kerse*s were used as jam-pots and the *ashourelik*s were used for offering a dessert based on wheat and dried fruit called *ashoure* in Turkish and *anoushabour* in Armenian. All these items of iridescent colours and curves constituted, as it were, a perfect symbiosis between Western art and the sweet things of the Orient.

"The furniture having to be very scanty," Marianne Damad continues, "luxury (…) blossomed in the costumes and the jewels. One cannot imagine the richness and the exquisite taste deployed in all that touched on finery and ornamentation: all sorts of embroideries, precious stones, gold, delightful settings of necklaces and rings. Here was to be seen an art of incomparable variety and splendour of the imagination."

As for the *yali*s, those at Therapia and Buyuk Dere, which had belonged to the Yaghoub and Sehpos Amiras – the two main Amiras at the start of the 18th century – they became respectively the summer residences of the Ambassadors of France and Russia. Later on, the *yali* of Megerdich Amira Djezahirli became the Austro-Hungarian Embassy.

* Armenian version of the Turkish kiassé.

About the *yalis* and their owners, we have a description emanating from a Mekhitarist of Venice, Father Luke Indjidjian, well-known in Armenian circles of the capital, chaplain for some, professor for others. Entitled "Byzantine Holidays", he published in 1794, in the city of the Doges, a narrative from which we quote eleven quatrains:

The Amiras possess enchanted places for the contemplation of
The Bosphorus and its summer resorts,
But they have no heart
To admire the work of the Creator.
The virtues of morality
Curb of unbridled passions,
Are strangers to their vain reckonings
On the elixirs prolonging life.
They wear finery to adorn their persons,
But they are not the ornament.
They refuse the virtues of morality,
Which alone adorn man.
Some, overwhelmed with the superfluous,
Complain of not having the essential.
Hunger and thirst for everything, jealousy towards anyone,
Showing something they do not possess already.
They complain of not having what they possess,
Because they do not enjoy the possessions they own.
By way of possessions, they have insatiable desires,
They do not dominate their possessions but are dominated by
their desire.
In a caïque I followed the sea that borders the town,
I saw the summer houses
Beautiful, superb, stretching out along the shore
And whose masters seem to have everything to make them happy.
I entered these residences to wander through them one after the other,
I examined their condition, their interior decoration.
I went in feeling happy, without the least sorrow,
I came out distressed, bitter and sad,
For the misfortunes I heard grieved me,
As also the plaintive mournings of each.
I thought I would be amused listening to their remarks,
I was, and they too, distressed to hear them.

One complained of the attitude of a friend,
Another of the snare set by an adversary,
A third of the unfair dealings of a debtor,
The last of the fees of a tenant.
They are willing to show their domains
But do not hesitate to recite their complaints.
The relative falls out with his relative,
The friend betrays the friend.
The husband denounces the laziness of the spouse,
The spouse, the severity of the husband,
The brother, the faults attributed to his brother,
The older blames the younger and the younger the older.

Another Mekhitarist of Venice, Father Manuel Chakhchakhian, has left us a still more scathing satire. His verses, composed in 1825 and published in 1852, seem to present a certain number of clues:

Some throng in scattered order on the Bosphorus of Thrace,
Building palaces or seeking the sensual delight of the zephyr.
Others show off in gilded speedy barques,
Yet others fill ancient pitchers with chrysolites.
Some watch wrestlers in the large valleys
Or contemplate tournaments huddling together…
What is the word in fashion? What are these bows, what are these embroideries?
Clothes from India and decorated with sable fur, rich and enviable.
The prizes of the contests are handed out in the street: a flute that the idle pass, by day, from hand to hand while exchanging greetings.
In the evening, nard or hashish always profoundly inhales,
Plunge them into a mindless state, into mental confusion.
Another, effeminate, is seated beside his prince charming
And his valiant heart continues to pour out his simpering love.
His hand stirs and shakes a stick of tobacco…
One also often sees an ass crowned with a gilt cushion,
Blinded by the branches that the witty wave on the hill,
Where one contemplates Andromeda like a ballet of stars
Whose body floating on the sea one sometimes beats.
Thus do they spend their life, believing it to be always a festivity,
Considering that in this way they are completely happy.
Just as the ignorant silk worms are enclosed in their narrow nests,

There are to be found their cradles and there their burial places always alive.

However much the blame and mistakes they castigate, the authors of these texts exaggerated like all Savonarolas or other Torquemadas. They pretend to ignore, purely and simply, that the Amiras of the 18th century were far from being mere sybarites. They overlook the fact that many of them were renowned for their piety, their virtues, for their love of God and their neighbours, for their charity. They even go so far as to make no mention of an essential criterion of the life of the Amira which bore witness to an undeniable nobility of mind.

Let us recall the reading, devout and constant, of the ardent stanzas of Gregory of Nareg, the greatest mystic of medieval Armenia (944–1010) of which we here cite an extract of the eleventh prayer particularly appreciated by the Amiras:

Now, because, I take refuge in this so luminous confidence,
destroyed, I remain standing;
stricken down, I am victorious;
lost, I take the invigorating path back;
the most miserable criminal, I live in hope;
abandoned to death, I remain alive,
become the prey to corruption, I am rewarded with incorruptibility;
besieged by infernal works, I live in light;
infatuated with petty things and an animal's life, I live in heaven;
relapsing into error, I still hope for salvation;
bounded by sin, I believe in the promise of rest;
anguished by incurable wounds,
I possess the remedy that makes one immortal;
untamed and wild, I am mastered by the bit that calms;
a vagrant and in flight, I head for the call;
stubborn and violent, I become gentle;
I who vilify and curse, I let myself go to forgiveness.
All this comes about thanks to Jesus Christ
and to his strong and redoubtable Father,
in the name and at the salutary will of the Spirit of truth.

It is well known that the Amiras read a great deal. Reading was one of their favourite pastimes. But what else did they read other than Gregory of

Nareg? They liked to read and re-read the bible in its beautiful 5th century Armenian translation. They also read the psalms, the lives of the Saints, the commentaries of the Holy Books, the Ephemerides and the monumental "History of Armenia" by the Mekhitarist Father Mikael Chamchian (1738–1823) who wrote the first Armenian history of modern times. Does not this preference for readings nourished by piety and history show that the culture of the Amiras resembles that of the well-read people of the Middle Ages?

They were so impregnated with the divine that they invoked it constantly, in an almost automatic way, punctuating their existence with calls on the Lord, some imploring, others triumphant. How often did one not see an Amira, seated on a divan, now bowing his head in a movement of contrition murmuring the most humble of *Der voghormia* ("Kyrie Eleison") and now lifting his eyes to heaven to give thanks in a vibrant voice: *Park kez Der im*? ("Glory to Thee, Lord").

These tokens of piety went hand in hand with a strong fascination for the refinements of the Osmanli *savoir-vivre*. Indeed, the Amiras were particularly sensitive to the charm of court Turkish, embellished by extensive borrowings from Arabic and Persian whose sumptuous intonations enhanced still further the pomp of the Osmanli ceremonial. In Turkish there are words conjuring up an art and easy way of life highly appreciated by the Amiras. The epithet *kibar* is one of the most beautiful words of the Turkish language. It designates all that encompasses the elegance of a gesture, the nobility of a thought; it is the mark of distinction. And all the refinement of the life at the Osmanli court is reflected therein.

In the Turkish vocabulary there is also a particularly pleasant word which, moreover, evokes pleasure; it is *keif*, marked with an untranslatable charm expressing a discrete pleasure, an agreeable entertainment, an acceptable sensual delight, inspired by the sight of a pretty woman or a beautiful object, a sweet sensation or a delicate pleasure, the company of agreeable society, the flavour of an exquisite dish, the bouquet of a good wine, in other words the love of life rather than love itself.

One of the summits of the *keif* consisted in the pleasure given by the puffs drawn from the *chibouks* that the smokers, seated in a circle with the hearth of their pipes placed on the floor, smoked in religious silence. Servants were specially assigned to the lighting and upkeep of there precious calumets, inseparable from the Ottoman way of life, whose attraction the Amiras had been unable to resist.

They adored everything which closely or remotely concerned the *salamaleks* of the Ottoman world. A simple exchange of *teshekürederim*[*] and *stafola*[†] overwhelmed them. But they relished equally the Armenian answers to the Turkish courtesy, which they repeated endlessly from dawn to dusk: *shnorhagal em*[‡] and *gaghachem.*[**]

While on this subject, let us underline the striking parallel between the Armenian *antsadz ulla* and the Turkish *gechmish olsoun* ("may it belong to the past," a formula used to congratulate a patient who has recovered from an illness) as between the Armenian *anoush ullah* and the Turkish *afiyet olsun* ("may it be agreeable to you," a compliment greeting the sweetness of a dish).

Ottoman etiquette was coupled with an inter-Armenian ritual giving the Amiras the most high-flown titles. Let us cite the examples of a bishop who, having to address an important request to an Amira (Djanig Amira Papazian), consulted a professor and asked him what was the most distinguished honorary expression. "Do you wish to write 'Amira of superb glory'" suggested the master. "That is not enough," replied the prelate. "'To the supreme glory,'" added his interlocutor, with a touch of irony in his voice, when he heard, "It's not enough... I've got it: put 'Dazzling Amira.'"[††]

The Fall of the Amiras (1860–1866)

About twenty years before they lost power, the Amiras appeared to have reached the height of their success. They conceived, in full agreement with the government, a spectacular banking set-up of unprecedented importance in Turkey. That was in 1842. Most astonishing, within the framework of this undertaking, the Amiras seemed, for the first time perhaps in their history, to be desirous to regroup and get on together, willing to unite rather than do each other harm! Thus, an all powerful institution was created uniting two banking companies, one called the "Company of Anatolia," the name for Asiatic Turkey and the other the "Company of Roumelia," the name for European Turkey. Together they became the *Anadoulou ve Rumeli*

---

* Teshekürederim *(Ott. Tur.):* Thank you.

† Stafola *(Ott. Tur.):* Don't mention it.

‡ Shnorhagal em *(Arm.)*: Many thanks.

** Gaghachem *(Arm.):* It's a pleasure (*lit.* I beg you).

†† In Armenian *Louassadjadjanch Amira.*

Kampanyasi, officially responsible, on the one hand, for the now centralized collection of all the revenues of the Empire, and, on the other hand, for financial incentives to be lavished on encouraging commercial development throughout the Ottoman territories. Each of these two companies was headed by a board of directors composed respectively of six Amiras – the whole being presided by Artin Amira Yerganian – the brother of the only Islamised Amira, on whom Sultan Abdul-Medjid conferred the *Iftiḥar* medal, set with diamonds, granting him and the eleven other Amiras the privilege of decorating their *fez* with a golden *toughra.**

These Amiras were amongst the most illustrious of their time and their names deserve mention:

Company of Anatolia;
- Artin Amira Yerganian
- Bedros Amira Kurkdjikhanli
- Missak Amira
- Megerdich Amira Djezahirli
- Baghdassar Amira Cherazian
- Boghos Ashnan

Company of Roumelia
- Djanig Amira Papazian
- Maxoud Amira (brother of the above)
- Artin Amira Guelguelian
- Abraham Amira Allahverdi
- Ohannes Amira Tinguir
- Hovsep Amira Davoudian (the last three were Catholic)

Now this institution, inaugurated with much ado and apparently destined for a brilliant future, did not live up to any of its expectations. It collapsed like a house of cards and was quickly forgotten. Did this prove, once and for all, that the union of the Amiras could only be an illusion even though their power could have been so much greater had they been able to sacrifice their quarrels for their interests?

To tell the truth, the deep reason for such a downfall remain obscure. We know neither the exact circumstances nor even the date. A timid allusion was made to an archaic management of finances. Even words such as

* Toughra (*Ott. Tur.*): Seal of the reigning sultan.

irregularities and abuse were murmured. We only know that this failure evidently did not benefit the Amiras but rather hastened its fall.

However, the decline of Armenian high finance did not result solely from internal dissensions between the Amiras, nor from their conservatism. It was due to other causes.

Firstly, to an economical cause. Banking ceased to be the basis of their power once the European banks, in particular the British, set foot in Turkey. Their modern management had superseded the financial monopoly of the Amiras, especially in transactions involving gold, pearls and precious stones.

Secondly, an Armenian cause. The Amiras were dispossessed, with regard to the Patriarchate, of the political prerogatives considered henceforth despotic. Such was the decision of the new class of Armenians who had been educated in France and obtained the grant of a new Constitution from Abdul-Aziz in 1863 to govern Armenian national life. A posthumous revenge of Megerdich Amira Djezahirli...

Finally, a Turkish cause. In 1840, the promulgation of the *Tanzimat* by Abdul-Medjid (supposedly) to establish equality between Muslims and non Muslims of the Empire and to allow minorities to earn such Turkish titles as Bey, Pasha, and Effendi, rendered the title of Amira obsolete. At the beginning of this book we saw that the Amiras became bankers by obligation rather than by vocation. Thus, when the occasion arose, they willingly abandoned the Bank to occupy, or rather, to see their descendants occupy, important posts in diplomacy and the government of the Empire.

Christians were at last able to mount, at will, thoroughbred horses instead of travelling around on donkeys. At the same time the barrier of the costume, to which the Turks had attached such value, disappeared. Till then, they had reserved for themselves the fine furs and most sparkling silky and shimmering colours which they had to exchange, not without regret, for the egalitarian dark-coloured and strict-cut redingote, buttoned up to the neck. Also the grandiose *kalpaks* were replaced by the official and compulsory uniformity of the fez. With nearly a century's advance, Turkey was faced with a vestimentary revolution comparable to the one which Mustafa Kemal was to impose later.

In order to mark the different times and evolution of mentalities, the Amiras and their descendants were henceforth allowed to grow generous beards, following the example of the Turkish dignitaries. In doing so they lost in secret power what they gained in visible honours... Certain situations were inevitably striking, as can be seen on a photograph showing the grandson of Missak Amira, Hovsep Effendi Missak, Turkish Ambassador to the Hague, recognisable by his white waist coat, seated amidst his associates, all Turkish, almost all standing and, curiously, more or less all beardless.

Among the members of the Company of Anatolia, we have cited the name of Missak Amira. Let us here take the opportunity of saying a few words about this family which, also originating in Agn, split up between that town, Constantinople and Aleppo. Missak Amira (1793–1856) had been an important personality, though we have little information about him. One of his brothers, Kevork Amira, was the Director of Customs in Ottoman Lebanon. Here is a description of the pilgrimage to Jerusalem which he accomplished on April 15th 1850 "where he entered with great ceremony, preceded by numerous lancers on horseback, rolling of drums and volleys of firearms."[*] It is from such details, gathered here and there with some difficulty, that one can get an idea of the life-style of the Amiras.

This digression on Missak Amira cannot be closed without evoking the moving example of Agop Bey Enkserdjis, a Catholic, director of the purchases by the Palace of antique French furniture and, at the end of the reign of Napoleon III, Chargé d'Affaires of Turkey in France.

It must be pointed out that in the 19th century, the representatives of the Empire abroad wrote all their correspondence destined for their Minister in French and it is in French that he gave them his instructions.

On August 12th 1870, Agop Bey sent a handwritten dispatch to Nevris Pasha, in French, in which he gave his point of view on the French-German conflict. We give the following extract from the four-page long manuscript:

> All France is in a commotion due to the invasion by the Prussians, all Paris rises and places itself in a defensive position to repel the invasion (...) I hope, moreover, that this war will not last long, the few setbacks sustained by the French make them all rise and defend their territory (...) The enthusiasm of the French is at its peak, out of patriotism they would let themselves be killed to the last man rather than tolerate the presence of a stranger, it is exactly like the Turks who would let themselves be cut to pieces in order to repel those who dare invade their territory. Believe me, Excellency, peace will be signed not

* "History of Jerusalem" by Dikran Hayrabed Savalaniantz, published in 1893, in classical Armenian.

> in Paris, as the Prussians say, but in Berlin, or at least in Cologne if the neutral Powers intervene to stop the bloodshed. France must regain a part of her natural frontiers, the Rhine, and she will not accept a shameful peace otherwise her anger and her indignation will turn against the authorities.

The author of this letter was mistaken, alas. But his faith in France remains nonetheless touching. It can be said Agop Bey Enkserdjis died for France because he was one of the accidental victims of the "Day of the Barricades" in 1871.

Just another word on the Amiras: these personalities were not exempt from a certain "ambiguity" – the word is that of the great Armenologist Yves Ternon – in the sense that they divided themselves between the service and control of the Empire, and the domination and protection of Armenia.

Nonetheless, their merit remains, with regard to the country of their ancestors, in the fact that they were, for a while, the "referees" of the Ottoman game and guardians of Armenian tradition and faith. As such, they are worthy of being remembered and honoured in posterity.

Up to the twilight of the Empire their descendants continued to form the elite of Armenian society of Constantinople.

Sovereigns and cultured women

Before entering in detail upon the great Armenian families to which the Amiras belonged, and to end those pages devoted to their world, we should discuss the women of these families. It is often through the women that one recognizes the authenticity of an elite. Undoubtedly Armenian society of Constantinople was, in this context, particularly blessed. The following illustrates this point.

Let us recall the story of the ten-year old girl called Herica, the eldest daughter of Arakel Bey Dadian. In 1855 she was sent to the Ursuline convent school in Paris, where she discovered to her amazement that the convent rules forbade young girls to wash themselves properly, since they were obliged to take a bath clothed in their nightdress! One day, taking advantage of the absence of the supervising sister, she decided to take a real bath. But the sister returned too soon. Scandalized, raising her hands to heaven, she said, "But, my child, don't you know that your guardian angel is of masculine sex?" Herica later married the most illustrious Armenian of Persia, Prince Mirza Malcom Khan, who is credited with the power… of halting time. The following anecdote is said about him: when he was Minister of the Interior, one morning, at 11 o'clock, he was due to preside a ceremony at which he turned up at 1 o'clock in the afternoon. Seeing the crest-fallen look of the people who were waiting for him, he asked, "What is the matter, sirs? Look at your watches!" All indicated... eleven o'clock. It is a historical fact. There is no need to seek an explanation, let us be content to quote it and see therein, perhaps, a phenomenon of collective telepathy.

A few years later, in 1869, after attending magnificent festivities in Egypt, where the Khedive Ismail marked the opening of the Suez Canal, the Empress Eugénie came to Constantinople to inaugurate the French lycee at Galata Saray. The Empress entered the Bosphorus on board her private ship *L'Aigle,* which cast anchor at the entry of the sound. Sultan Abdul-Aziz, successor of Abdul-Medjid and, like him, favourable to Christians, was said to be smitten by Eugénie and came to meet her standing in the centre of his twelve-pair oared caïque. He led her at once to the superb palace at Beylerbey, the architectural jewel which the great architects Hagop and Sarkis Balian had just built. Madame Mihran Bey Duz, who had the pretty name of Marionka, was immediately assigned to the Empress as her lady in waiting and interpreter. She was the wife of the last Duz to have occupied the post of Director of the Imperial Mint.

Next day, Eugénie went, as protocol required, to pay a visit to the Sultana Validé.* Marionka, of course, accompanied her. According to the custom in the courts of Europe, the Empress wished to embrace the Sultana, who was unable to suppress a movement of recoil at that very moment and this cast a chill on the meeting. Numerous sweet dishes and liqueurs were served before coffee was brought, all of which Eugénie refused, much to the astonishment of the Validé, for whom this coffee ritual was one of the principals of Oriental hospitality. She wanted to know the reason for this refusal: "Oh, said the Empress, if I drink coffee, I'll climb on to the furniture." This sentence was never translated. Marionka just said, *Tadji zeler* which can be expressed as "it is harmful to her." Abdul-Aziz was told that the Validé had not wished to embrace the Empress. Furious, the Sultan

* The title of Sultana Validé was the right, like that of Highness, of the mother of the reigning Sultan, having become First Lady of the Empire after being the Imperial favourite.

scolded his mother. Taken aback by the expression of deep annoyance on her son's face, she tried to make up for her mistake. On the occasion of a further visit, Eugénie was surprised to see the Sultana throw her arms around her neck!

A generation later, what a stirring contrast Abdul-Hamid II, the Armenophobe, was to his father Abdul-Medjid, the reformer. Incredible as it may seem, the latter one day asked the Patriarch of Armenia to come to his sick mother's bedside to bless her and recite Christian prayers! A week later Sultana Validé was cured and she showered the Patriarch with gifts.

Between the end of the 19th century and the start of the 20th, three Armenian ladies held a literary salon in Constantinople, in the style of the French ladies of the 18th century. The order of precedence in which we cite them is that of age.

The first was Madame Kevork Effendi Aslan, née Dadian, who, in the absence of beauty possessed extreme charm and vivacity. She was called the "Pretty-Ugly," like the Princess of Metternich, wife of the Austrian Ambassador to the Court of Napoleon III. Her daughter Anna married Nagib Pasha Boutros-Ghali, uncle of the Secretary General to the United Nations.

The second was Madame Edgard Bey Duz, daughter of Ohhanes Effendi Allahverdi. An exceptional woman, of incomparable distinction, she saw all Constantinople pass through her salon, including diplomats and scholars. She was particularly fond of the Russian world. The Ambassador of the Tsar was a regular visitor at her receptions. She sometimes said, evidently not in his presence, "I adore the Russians; they are so brilliant, so decorative. I love to see them in my salon. But I would give neither my purse not my heart to a Russian." She admired Pierre Loti, who saw her assiduously and placed her, under an assumed name, in one of his novels. One day he published a book in which he denigrated Armenia in favour of Turkey. Outraged, Madame Duz wrote him a letter of remonstration and closed the door on him. She spoke French of a rare quality, the French of the 18th century, with a flavour enhanced by the singing intonation of Pera, that connoisseurs call the Perote accent. And, when she spoke in Armenian, it seemed as if one heard the admirable but unintelligible language of Krikor Naregatsi or Nerses Shnorhali, great mystics of medieval Armenia...

The third of these cultivated ladies, and no doubt the most literate of the three, a granddaughter of Arakel Bey Dadian – always the same circle – was Madame Gabriel Effendi Servicen, née Astiné Vahan, a caustic and passionate woman, who was called the blue-stocking of Constantinople.

Mme Naguib Pasha Boutros-Ghali (1885–1984)

After the Armistice of Moudros, on October 30th 1918, marking the capitulation of the Ottoman Empire and the entry of the Allies into the imperial capital, several French officers asked to meet the Armenian society of the city. Later on, a number of them married some of their daughters. It is thus that the future Admiral de Ravenel married Mlle Yaghoubian; Baron Sérot-Alméra-Latour, Mlle Eram; Count Patrimonio, Mlle Esmerian, etc... Why not see in these marriages a strategy of survival, due as much to affinities as to attractions of the fifty of so marriages concluded from the 11th to the 14th century, between the French and Armenian nobility?

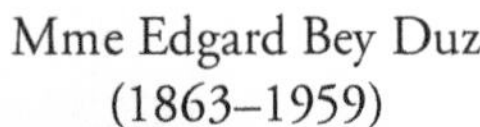

Mme Edgard Bey Duz (1863–1959)

In honour of these officers Madame Servicen organised a large reception during which the young and brilliant Hermine Aslan made the conquest of Colonel (and shortly to become General) Borivérier, who asked to meet her mother. Madame Artin Effendi Aslan was in mourning (for her husband). "Oh well," she said to her daughter, "for one day we shall go out of mourning." For a few hours the splendours of the time of Artin Effendi were resuscitated. When the Colonel arrived at

Alleon Street and saw Madame Artine Effendi waiting for him at the top of the staircase of honour surrounded by such elegance, he had to exclaim, "Madam, one would think we were at the Faubourg Saint Germain." This flattering statement marked the swan-song of the patricians of Ottoman Armenia.

Mme. and Artin Effendi Aslan (1869–1965)

Madame Servicen was the daughter-in-law of the famous Doctor Servicen, who was both the friend of the Grand-Vizier Ali Pasha and one of the most generous "maîtres à penser" of young Armenians just back from France and eager for progress and renewal.

In Paris, where he had studied medicine, the future Doctor Servicen had a liaison with the daughter of his caretaker. When he learnt that she was pregnant, he immediately decided to marry her. In doing so he gave, according to some people, a great example of "Armenian honour." It is important to remember that, once settled in Constantinople, the pretty little French woman knew perfectly well how to maintain her rank. She gave birth to Gabriel Effendi Servicen, future Ottoman high civil servant.

Much later, I myself visited Madame Servicen who, like Madame Duz, was four times my age. I was twenty at the time and deeply admired these ladies who embodied the glory of French Armenia. One day, pointing with a large gesture at the small two-roomed flat at Square de Thimerais, which was all that remained of her former splendour, the so-called blue-stocking said, "Paul Valéry is my god and this house is his temple." Her daughter, Louise Servicen, had been the distinguished translator of Thomas Mann into French.

These few pages have been purposely marked above all with a feminine touch, thus rendering homage to the Armenian ladies of Constantinople who, more than a century ago, in the heart of the Orient, set a great example of emancipation *à la française* and a refined image of women.

5

The Great Families

The Momdjians

Sarkis Amira Momdjian (1750–1818) and his twin brother Arakel Amira (1750–1832) are at the origin of a family of scholars and philanthropists. The first of the two was a Banker Prince in all his splendour. Like many of his peers, besides banking, he was involved in many activities which, though subsidiary, were nonetheless important. It was thus that, amongst other privileges, Sarkis Amira had the monopoly of wax which made him the exclusive supplier to the Sublime Porte of candles and other lighting substances, ensuring him a significant source of income.

He and his family owned four palaces in stately Haskeoy, situated each side of a private alley guarded by *bekdjis*.* Built in a homogenous style, with an abundant use of marble imported from Carrara, these *konaks* stood out on the Golden Horn and comprised an estate which included other palaces belonging to the cousins of Sarkis Amira, notably that of Agop Amira Latif (1750–1833) and his son Ohannes Amira, (1770–1859).

Let us describe a reception given by Sarkis Amira at the end of the 18th century. In fact, the term reception is inappropriate. The word banquet is more suitable, in Armenian, *khundjouyk*.

Sarkis Amira received his peers and followers – and no doubt the excellent Father Luke whose satires amused him – clad in a purple cloak edged with ermine. He looked very distinguished as the master of ceremonies. His son, Ohannes Momdjian (1770–1822), assisted him in welcoming the guests. Each arrival gave rise to an exchange of deep bows with the hand placed on the forehead.

A sideboard of imposing dimensions, covered with exquisite dishes, was placed in the centre of the banqueting hall. The Aghabani tablecloth, woven in spun gold, the glint of silver goblets, the wines sparkling in Bohemian glass decanters, and the white and blue patterns of the famous Kutahya plates created a most effective lustre. If the blend of blue and white had been the pride of the potters from the time of the Chinese splendours of the Ming Dynasty to the azulejos of the Iberian Peninsula and the glazed earthenware of

* Bekdji (*Ott. Tur.*): Guards.

Rouen or Delft, Turkey was equally renowned for the Iznik and Kutahya factories whose artists were often Armenian.

No woman, according to Turkish custom, was present amongst the guests; the female sex was nonetheless represented by dancers hired for the occasion and danced less with their legs than with their arms and hands, weaving gracious arabesques around themselves. In one corner there was an orchestra playing string instruments similar to viola da gambas. Tambourines were also used to beat out the Turkish rhythm of the *indjesaz*[*] of which the men were very fond.

That evening Sarkis Amira introduced sumptuous cutlery ordered from France and wrought in Damascus. Of original design, these knives, forks and spoons were made of pewter, in Louis XVI style, and encrusted with Islamic motifs in gold. Yet another illustration of the encounter between Orient and Occident, engraved in letters of gold by Armenia!

The feast was in full swing. Whole quarters of mutton were speared on enormous spits. The dancers twirled, the waiters bustled, the dishes were delectable and the wines delicious. The sacrosanct coffee ritual announced the end of the meal. A horde of turbaned waiters brought the coffee on trays covered in lace and served in *findjans*[†] placed on *zarfs*.[‡] These objects were accompanied by one or two *komkoms* (in English, sprinklers) in either early 18th century Chinese porcelain or 19th century Bohemian opalines, twenty to thirty centimetres high. They were flasks of a somewhat curious shape, rounded at the base with a very fine neck, and were used to flavour the coffee by the addition of a few drops of rose or orange water. Some specimens of these *komkoms* can be seen in the admirable Topkapi Palace Museum today.

The dinner ended with the equally traditional jam ritual, brought on still larger trays, and carried by two servants wearing *shalvars*.[**] The jam was presented in *kerses*, those beautiful spherical objects designed for Constantinople. The *kerses* were accompanied by two spoon-holders, one containing spoons before use, the other after use. Spoon-holders and spoons were marvels in silver plate.

---

* Turkish folklore music.

† Small cup with no handle, in Dresden china or Chinese porcelain called *Têtes de Turcs* [Turks' heads] in French.

‡ Objects resembling silver egg-cups, very often in filigree or interlaced design.

** Shalvar (*Ott. Tur.*): Large, baggy trousers.

These feasts, which obviously bore the mark of Turkish influence, also had a medieval touch. Half a century later, medieval and Turkish manners began to fade away on contact with French culture.

The epitaph on the tombstone of the munificent Sarkis Amira is worth noting. Through the serene piety and the simplicity of the inscription pierces the pride of the Amira:

EPITAPH OF SARKIS AMIRA MOMDJIAN
1750–1818
Approach this tomb, oh beloved who passeth by,
And read what was my destiny,
Born in the town of Agn,
The race of the Momdjians have I continued,
When baptised I was called Sarkis,
Of noble Marcos I am the son.
Having reached my sixty-eight year,
At the prime of old age, I keep watch in this dwelling,
Where I await the return of the Saviour,
Hoping by your prayers His pity.
In the year of the Lord 1818

22nd February.
Constantinople
(Translated from classical Armenian)

Between the years 1825 and 1835, Abraham Momdjian, the grandson of Sarkis Amira, recorded the births of his six children on thin sheets of parchment: Sarkis, Ohannes, Nectar (who only survived eight days), Artin, Nectar (the future Madame Mikael Momdjian), Stepan, each birth being accompanied by a noble and pious wish written in beautiful classical Armenian: *Der Astvadz zharank pari arastse yev shnorhok zarkatsoustse.* (That the Lord grant him happiness and endow him with Grace).

The great-grandson and homonym of Sarkis Amira, Sarkis Momdjian (1825–1890) worried his family regarding family conformity. One afternoon in 1845, the brilliant spring sun flooded the Bosphorus whose waves, palaces and boats were mingled in a blaze impossible to describe. At the centre of these fireworks appeared the superb Madame Momdjian surrounded by followers who crossed the straits on board her caique. This kind of gondola, in Constantinople style, whose elegance owes as much to its splendid shape as to the grace of its movement, was manoeuvred by several oarsmen – the *kayikdjis* – who made their caiques glide on the crest of the waves. Suddenly Madame Momdjian retched; she had just learnt, from one of her companions, that her eldest son had fallen in love with a young girl whose image corresponded neither to her vision of propriety nor to the criteria of her family. Madame Abraham Momdjian was a very unusual personality. Married to the grandson of Sarkis Amira Momdjian, and herself the daughter of the powerful Alpiar Amira, she had the right to be called *Hanoum Doudou*, a respectful expression whose two components, borrowed from Turkish, each signifying "Madame." This juxtaposition was homage to the patrician – her own children calling her "Doudou" according to the custom observed at that time by the sons of good families – and underlining at the same time the noble and authoritative character of a woman for whom existing and dominating were one and the same thing. It was therefore out of the question for such a woman to allow her son to behave so lightly in such a fundamental domain as marriage.

On what were Hanoum Doudou's apprehensions based? Did she fear a misalliance? A relationship between equal but rival families? A breach of honour? We do not really know, especially because we still do not know the identity, jealously guarded, of the person arousing such agitation amongst the Momdjians.

In Constantinople, the notion of misalliance was not always considered, as it was in Europe: a breach of family equilibrium. A marriage between partners of the same social status was certainly considered desirable, but the thirst for power, the undivided individualism and hostility towards their peers, which, alas, was so characteristic of the Amiras, quite often ruined all hope of concluding matrimonial truces between the young of the same world but often a world torn apart.

When such was the case, the family in search of a daughter-in-law chose what was conventionally called "honourable humility." This transparent formula referred to young girls of modest origins, the most sought after candidates being recruited from the lower clergy, among the daughters of priests. Such girls were expected to have received a pious education and to promise total submission to their powerful in-laws.

These examples show that within a society steeped in convention, the preparation for marriage was left neither to chance nor to improvisation. It gave rise, sometimes for years, to family mediations, calculations and arrangements, meticulously organizing in secret meetings the destiny of couples who were directly affected by these decisions but the last to know each other. The bride and bridegroom had to wait until their ceremony to see each other, when the bridegroom unveiled the face of the bride, according to a set ritual based on Turkish customs.

Woe betide those who wished to break away from such constraints! A marriage which was not prepared according to the rituals of a very strict tradition could be considered a "misalliance." Hence, perhaps, an explanation for the wrath of Hanoum Doudou, which the privations of Lent carried to an extreme. In fact, during the forty days of fasting Hanoum Doudou, as an act of contrition, only ate dry bread and black olives! In his *Grand Dictionnaire Historique*, published in 1694, Louys Morery wrote in this connection, that "in the Oriental Church there is no people giving more importance to fasting than Armenians, and it seems normal that they make all their religion lie therein."

Before making any decision, Hanoum Doudou wanted to meditate a short while. She ordered the oarsmen to return to Haskeoy and went to the private beach bordering the palace of the Momdjians on the Golden Horn. Let us digress a moment to say that Hanoum Doudou, for some unknown reason, forbade her children to be seen on the beach, even a private one. For their baths she had large buckets of sea water brought to her residence. For the time being she tried to make her son listen to reason. But as young Sarkis did not give in – his twenty years only strengthening his determination – she decided to take strong action. Considering her husband to be too accommodating, she called on her father, one of the most austere of the Amiras of the time, and begged him to take the necessary steps to avoid the worst before it was too late. One made no bones about such matters in those families and the decision taken was draconian: not only was the unrepentant lover to be separated from the object of his passion, but he was to be exiled to distant Arabia to meditate on his behaviour, for which he was blamed, and return to a sounder idea of permitted love, which required a long penitence.

Contrary to expectations, the traveller, in spite of himself, did not choose to revolt. He was provided with a cart yoked to three oxen, a driver and a valet, and it was thus that the heir to the Momdjians set off on the inexorable road to Arabia, which he had to cover rapidly to obey the orders he had received. The regions they passed through were picturesque but the journey exhausting, full of the unavoidable pitfalls of the Turkish roads of the time. This virtual banishment to the heart of a lost region was to last for many lengthy years during which the hapless Sarkis waited patiently for the exile to end. It seems that he nevertheless made the best of it without too much trouble, thanks to his happy nature, which enabled him to organize life in a kind of oasis.

This ostracism lasted no less than twenty years, after which those in high places decided that a rare chance, a granddaughter of an Amira, was suited to become his wife and he her husband. He was then authorized to return home.

In a final gesture of defiance of his family, on his return to Haskeoy, the prodigal son was accompanied by a negress with the looks of a goddess. Servant or mistress? We have no idea. We only know that the unknown beauty was dismissed on the spot.

After this final folly, family ties got the upper-hand and Sarkis – now Sarkis Agha – became an irreproachable Momdjian, faithful husband and model father. But, prior to this, he had to submit, without complaining, to the very special ceremonial of a marriage celebrated in great pomp in the church of Haskeoy, inundated with flowers and crowded with people. Wearing a crinoline dress and a lace headdress Hanoum Doudou relished her triumph. As for the bride, she waited impatiently to discover the man who was to be her husband and who, with the same impatience, awaited the moment he would accomplish his very personal gesture: the removal of the veil that covered a still unknown bride from head to foot. After observing this ritual, they exchanged a furtive glance in silence, as social convention demanded. It was a look full of meaning and of great mutual relief. From this instant the bride became Rosik Hanoum and all were able to admire the grace of her sixteen years and the still secret charm of the now blossoming beauty.

"*Momdjonts harsn e*" (She's the daughter-in-law of the Momdjians) was for weeks and even months after this wedding the murmurs of admiration from the benches reserved for members of the great families in the church of Haskeoy, as Rosik Hanoum arrived at Sunday Mass. In fact, this marriage, which took place in 1865, was to be one of the last great Armenian marriages to observe these customs. The evolution of ideas, to which Sarkis Agha was no stranger, occurred more rapidly than might have been expected. The mutual ignorance of each other, which was nothing less than a violation of the dignity of the young couples, was perceived more and more as the survival of a formal Ottoman universe.

These practices of another age became obsolete around 1870, when the Amiras lost the right to lord over morals, at the same time as they saw their political power melt away. The "match-makers," previously so influential, also saw their power fade away. Though arranged marriages may still have taken place, they no longer exceeded the limits of freely consented proposals.

Sarkis Momdjian (1825–1890)

In conclusion, we can say that the cornerstone of such a demanding system was largely due to the dissensions between Amiras and the implacable rivalries which complicated matrimonial interplay. These factors came to an end after the descendants of Amiras, at last freed from the necessity to flee rival families, could freely unite according to their affinities and tastes without internal struggles and forced marriages.

One should not be astonished at the intransigence or severity shown by the world of the Amiras. The Momdjians, well known for the quality of their education and culture as well as their very refined manners and kindness could, without ceasing to be courteous, become implacable as soon as their code of honour or their *savoir-vivre* was violated.

Ohannes Momdjian, younger brother of Sarkis, got into difficulties in an affair similar to that which had overshadowed the youth of his elder brother, but showing himself less docile and therefore incorrigible, he was banished forever from the family circle. As for the two youngest, Djanig and Stepan, they considered it wiser to remain single – just like the two younger brothers of their father – and were all the more appreciated. But their "wisdom" was due to a resignation that finally destroyed all initiative.

The worrying inactivity of his brothers touched Sarkis Agha who decided to provide them with an occupation. Within the context of the time and place, the office of Banker was, we know, highly thought of. So be it! In

1876, Sarkis Agha founded an opulent bank and gave the reins to the two idlers. With the prestige of their name, this bank became one of the most popular rendez-vous of elegant Constantinople. The two brothers quickly made a fortune and became bankrupt still more rapidly, ruining not only themselves but also their families.

If the Amiras could be implacable, they could also be admirable. Family severity had a corollary: family solidarity. This disaster – which the proud Hanoum Doudou did not survive – sounded the death-knell of their fortune but not of the honour of the Momdjians. Sarkis Agha reimbursed, to the last piastre, the debts accumulated by his brothers. Then, without a word, he left the ancestral home whose upkeep he was no longer able to afford. The Turkish government converted it into barracks.

Mikael Momdjian (–1894)

During the eight years following his return from Arabia and prior to this "debacle," Sarkis Momdjian, every Sunday at midday, opened his house and table to his numerous friends. The Patriarch of Constantinople, Mgr. Nerses, often enjoyed coming to preside at these meals, as did the venerable archpriest Kevork Ardzrouni, chaplain to all Haskeoy. The Patriarch, one day, declared during one of the Sunday feasts, that he very much hoped to bless the marriage of young Serpouhi (Sophie), daughter of the master of the house. The guests were unable to suppress their surprise, the person mentioned being only seven years old and the august old man having just reached ninety. Then a faint voice was heard from the other end of the table: "Father is too old. When I get married he'll be 'mot' (for 'mort' dead)." The future Madame Artin Effendi Aslan never forgot the scolding she received from her mother when the guests had left. It so happened that the old archpriest was true to his word. It was indeed he who blessed the union which he had so much at heart. On June 8th 1887, the wedding day of Serpouhi, aged 18, her father, who had now been ruined and lived in a small house in Scutari, went to fetch the archpriest at Haskeoy. When this very old man, aged one hundred and blind, clinging to the arm of Sarkis Momdjian entered the house,[*] all the assistants rose to their feet. The archpriest began by blessing the house using a censer, the magnificent incense burner which had belonged to the Momdjians for generations. Addressing first the bride's parents he said, "This child, I removed from the baptismal font to entrust to her father and mother. Today I am taking her back from the hands of her father and mother and – turning to the bridegroom – entrust her to you: are you worthy of her?" It was an exceptional moment and the witnesses were very moved. It should be explained that the marriage was sponsored by the Capitan Pasha,[†] the hierarchical superior of the bridegroom who was also his friend. But, as a Muslim, the Minister could not take an active part in a Christian marriage, where the "sponsor" is the main participant in a ceremony during which he has to hold a cross above the heads of the bride and bridegroom. This ritual takes on its full significance at the very moving moment when the two spouses bend their heads towards each other, forehead touching forehead, while a silk cord enlaces both of their necks.

Since such an important role could not be rightfully performed by a Turk, however high-ranking he might have been, the Minister delegated the role to his friend Ohannes Effendi Essayan[‡] who, considering himself too old for such a task, had in turn delegated it to his son Yervant Essayan, who acquitted himself to everyone's satisfaction.

At Haskeoy, in the palace nearest to the one which had belonged to Sarkis Momdjian, lived his brother-in-law and cousin Mikael Momdjian. The latter, every inch a patrician, could be scathing to an almost reckless degree, clashing head-on with Armenian conservatism. The premature loss, in Paris, of a niece beloved by all the Momdjians, inspired him, as if to thumb his nose at death, to address these words by way of condolences to the inconsolable widower: "Our loss is immense and terrible to the point of entitling us to start proceedings against destiny." No doubt he said "destiny" so as not to use the word "God," but this cry of revolt was nonetheless audacious given the fossilized world which combined the pre-eminence of faith to the dread of the hereafter.

* These marriages were celebrated either at home or in church.

† Permanent Minister of the Turkish Navy.

‡ Eminent benefactor of the Armenian Nation, to which he gave a College bearing his name.

The niece in question was called Nectar de Czunt (1842–1890), granddaughter of Nigoghos Momdjian (1777–1861), and sister of the poet Alixane Panossian, who was active in the Armenian ladies' charitable associations. She had married Déodat de Czunt (Chountian) (1825–1897) who, through his father, was a descendant of a family living in Polish Galicia since the 16th century. His mother was a member of the Von Prounkeul (Prounkoulian) family ennobled by the Empress Maria-Theresa of Austria.* Czunt settled in Constantinople where he was remembered as a generous patron particularly of schools. The Emperor François-Joseph made him a hereditary knight in 1875.

The Karakehias

The Karakehias, like the Momdjians, lived on the shores of the Golden Horn. Abraham Amira Karakehia (in Turkish "the black administrator") owed his name to his ancestor Abraham Kara Oghlou. This Abraham Amira (1767–1827) was one of the best-loved patricians of his time. He greatly contributed to the enrichment of the cultural heritage of his generation by printing historical and religious books which he endowed to the nation. It was he who, in his will, left the sum necessary for the reconstruction of the church of Haskeoy (1830) which occasioned the famous episode of the belfry protected by the Sultan.

On the eve of the 19th century Abraham Amira was visited by an ambitious soldier. The man, who was poorly clad but proud of his appearance, spoke in a language that was enhanced by the use of the familiar Oriental "you". "Lord, you are a powerful banker and I am not but a poor soldier. Will you risk part of your fortune in my favour? If I fail in my intentions you will never see your money again, but if I succeed, I will repay you a hundred times over. As a pledge, here is my watch, my only possession."

It was not unusual for Amiras to assist the rise of modest but worthy men likely to help them in return later on. In the present case Abraham Amira was charmed by the mixture of humility and boldness in the soldier. He refused the pledge and accepted the deal. He did not regret it. The visitor was none other than Mehmet Ali who, as soon as he had taken over Egypt

---

* Since the Middle Ages, several Armenian colonies were established in Central Europe, having fled the Turkish invasions. They kept their Armenian identity up to the 19th century.

– at the time an Ottoman province – looked to the Amira and his descendants to uphold the interests of the Viceroys of Egypt by attending the Sublime Porte with the title of *Missir sarafi*, Banker of Egypt.

The Karakehias distinguished themselves by the peculiarity of their ways and their tastes. The paradox persisted, be it in Constantinople or elsewhere. Without becoming Muslim, the Amiras could be Islamophiles. A typical example was the case of Garabed Bey Karakehia, nephew of Abraham Amira, who was particularly fond of the chants of the muezzins. Apparently one need not be a Muslim to appreciate the true value of the haunting chant of the call to prayer.

In order to fully enjoy the sensual pleasure of this call, Garabed Bey had the absurd idea of building, in the centre of his gardens, a small mosque, made to measure, cheerful and spruce, decorated with rich mosaics and undulating arabesques. He had shimmering carpets put down and the whole was capped with a graceful minaret served by an accredited muezzin, uttering talented nasal twangs or the sweetest of mooings for the ears of his lord and master. A surrounding of flowers and their perfume allowed him to relish even more the sweetness of the chants!

This infatuation for the voice and not the faith of Islam scarcely troubled Christian society, accustomed to the eccentricities of the Bey. Contrary to all expectations it was a Turkish mob which, furious at the "stain" cast on one of Allah's sanctuaries by an impure protection, burst into the Bey's park armed with pickaxes and destroyed the pretty mosque. They attacked in particular the minaret, the perfection of its form and the force of its power, guilty of having rung out a celestial chant too greatly appreciated by a profane person, who was also a music-lover.

Kevork Bey Karakehia, elder brother of Garabed Bey, thought it clever to betroth his youngest daughter, Zarouhi, to Krikor Odian, a rising figure in the new bourgeoisie and future father of the first Turkish constitution, which was turned down by Abdul-Hamid II. Odian possessed neither the prejudices nor the eccentricities of old society, but neither had he the class or prestige. He saw in this proposed union a way for his social ascent. He was invited to spend a few days at the palace of the Karakehias.

Very early one morning, the mistress of the house caught her future son-in-law in a secluded corner of the park, in the shade of the giant cedar trees, indulging in a strange exercise and an unusual attire: with bare feet and clad just in a night gown, a bonnet on his head and a shawl around his shoulders, he paced up and down a series of icy flagstones.

"I did not know you were such an early riser nor so fond of sport" said Madame Kevork Bey jokingly. "Oh, Hanoum Effendi," replied Odian somewhat embarrassed, "it is less a question of sport than a treatment borrowed from peasant wisdom, sometimes sounder than advanced medicine. The exercise that I am now doing is the only one that had proved sufficiently effective to enable me to counteract the chronic effects of an acute astringency." The familiarity of the remark could but make one smile, especially the Karakehias, who laughed at everything. But there they froze, like the flagstones in their park, and broke off the engagement… Krikor Odian no doubt lacked the distinction of his were-to-have-been in-laws, but the kind man and gifted thinker that he was did not deserve the social ostracism inflicted by the Karakehias.

As for the young Zarouhi, she lived for a long time after this event without ever getting married. Was she too independent? A long time afterwards, one afternoon in 1920, when already getting on in years, Zarouhi Hanoum was rowing alone in the lake of the Bois de Boulogne in Paris. Bedros Effendi Haladjian, the last Armenian Minister of the Ottoman Empire, went by chance to the Bois de Boulogne. Observing the scene and not thinking he could be heard, and still less understood, he asked the people with him, in Armenian "Who is that crazy person?" A scathing answer shot back from the boat, "I'm not mad. I am Zarouhi Karakehia," whereupon, the minister fled!

Well before this incident, Zarouhi and her mother, when travelling on the Orient Express, met a very ugly man. "Who can this monkey be?" Madame Kevork Bey asked her daughter in Armenian. "I'm not a monkey," replied the stranger in the same language…

From the middle of the 19th century Madame Kevork Bey had given up wearing Oriental dresses in Constantinople and had adopted the European style. One of her magnificent Oriental dresses, after being displayed at the Great Exhibition of Paris in 1867, was exhibited at the Louvre Museum, Pavillon de Marsan, for almost a century, entitled, "Armenian dress." Her daughter, Madame Ohannes Bey Dadian, willingly evoked for her granddaughters – one being Ann Boutros Ghali – her dresses by Worth (famous couturier of the Second Empire, launched by the Princess de Metternich, wife of the Austrian Ambassador), her hats from Virot, and the passionate interest of the ladies of her time for the fashions set by the Empress Eugenie.

Abraham Pasha Karakehia, son of Kevork Bey, last Karakehia to have represented the Viceroy of Egypt at the Court of Constantinople, was an important but enigmatic personality. Very close to Abdul-Aziz (the last armenophile Sultan), he retained his position during Abdul-Hamid's rule as senator for life and State Councillor before being raised to the rank of Vizier.* It is relevant to know that he had a very pretty wife and was extremely jealous.

One evening in 1884 Abraham Pasha gave a large ball in his superb *yali* at Buyuk-Dere – "the Great Valley" in Turkish – on the edge of the Bosphorus. It was a brilliant party with all Constantinople thronging there, but strangely enough, the signal for the start of the dancing was long in coming. Astonished, the Marques of Noailles, wife of the French Ambassador, approached a young guest, Nectar Allahverdi, and asked her, "My child, wouldn't you like to dance?" The young lady, who would shortly become the dazzling Madame Edgar Bey Duz, replied, "Oh yes Madame" with a gracious smile. "I'll go and speak about it to the master of the house," decided Madame de Noailles. "My Pasha," she said to him, "the young people would like to dance." "Yes, Madame, I share this wish," declared the Pasha, "but I am just waiting, before opening the ball, for His Beatitude to take leave." The prelate mentioned was the Patriarch of Constantinople, Mgr. Nerses Varjabedian. However, His Beatitude did not retire because the Pasha had asked him not to leave the party, so that the ball could not take place, so that his wife did not dance.... thus ended a deceptive ball, a dance without dancers.

Apart from such anecdotes, the Karakehias remained the "Bank of Egypt" and defended of the interests of the Viceroy (a title borne by Mehemet Ali and his descendants who were also Pashas).

Mehemet Ali owed as much to Abraham Amira as to his own genius for his amazing success. On becoming master of Egypt, he discovered that the coffers of the Vice-regency were empty. He asked for loans. Only Yeghiazar Amira Bedrossian granted him his confidence. Staring at him with his jet-black eyes he declared that "he put his purse and his life at the disposal of the Pasha." The Viceroy made him the administrator of what was then called the Private Treasury (Finance Minister).

---

* Not to be confused with Grand-Vizier (Prime Minister).

In order to understand Mehemet Ali's fondness for Armenians, one must never forget that at the beginning he owed his success to two Amiras, the first from Istanbul and the second from Cairo. But his Armenian sympathies went still further. Determined to be absolute master of Egypt and a purely nominal vassal of the Sultan, he removed the Mameluks from power and placed Armenians at key posts in his government. It was the first time that, on Ottoman territory, Christians acceded to political functions. The chief of these Armenians was Boghos Youssoufian. He was a descendant of Abro Chelebi who, as we have already mentioned, was a precursor of the Amiras. He was also the first Armenian to receive the title of Bey. He ran five ministries simultaneously, the main ones being those of Foreign Affairs and Commerce. He had great influence on the Egyptian Pasha and assumed the functions of a Prime Minister.

That the Pasha favoured Armenians can be seen by his desire to surround himself with reliable men who were totally devoted to him and posed no threat to his power. Armenians were open to the West and the reforms he wished to introduce while they were also familiar with Turkish society, whose language they spoke. The Viceroy had imposed Turkish as the official language of the Egyptian administration. Paradoxically, he preferred to express himself in Turkish despite wanting to emancipate Egypt from Turkish influence.

The open-mindedness towards the West took the form of dispatching young men of good families to France in order to acquaint them to French culture. Bogos Bey was the person responsible for sending them off and was thus, for Egypt, what Djezahirli had been for Turkey, except that Djezahirli acted as a sponsor and Boghos as a Minister.

The most brilliant of these students was the young Armeno-Catholic Artin Chrakian, future Minister of Foreign Affairs, appointed on his return from France as interpreter to the Viceroy. The latter, who appreciated Chrakian's qualities, asked him for a Turkish version of *The Prince.* Considering himself to be Machiavelli, Mehemet Ali particularly valued the mixture of tolerance and cunning in Chrakian.

Artin set to work translating ten pages a day. When he had reached the fortieth page, the Pasha, bored of reading, said to the translator: "Not having discovered anything new in the first ten pages, I hoped to find something better in the following ones. But the next ten were scarcely better and the last ones commonplace. It is obvious that I have nothing to learn from

Machiavelli. With regard to cunning, I know more than Machiavelli. It is useless to translate any more."*

When Mehemet Ali took up arms against his ruler, he was unable to overthrow the Sultan because of the intervention of the European powers, but it was the diplomacy of Boghos Bey that saved his skin and his throne.

No less extraordinary is the fact that when the Viceroy endangered the Sultan and the Empire (1831), Eram Amira Karakehia (1768–1853), brother and successor of Abraham Amira, was not bothered, whereas ten years earlier the rebellion of the Pasha of Jannina cost the life of Cheraz Amira. This immunity was due as much to the evolution of the Ottoman regime as to the prestige of the Karakehias.

Finally, Nubar, nephew of Boghos, was the first Armenian – and first Christian – to receive the title of Pasha, a great distinction in Egypt, where he was the Minister of Foreign Affairs and Prime Minister. Many books have been written about him and his biography fills several pages of the *Encyclopedia of the 19th Century.* Nubar Pasha was the best known of Armenian politicians of modern times. His marriage, sponsored by Megerditch Amira Djezahirli, was to the eldest daughter of Kevork Bey Karakehia.

Prince Tigrano d'Abro, Minister of Foreign Affairs and Nubar's son-in-law and great-nephew of Boghos, ended the dynasty of Armenian statesmen who governed Egypt in the 19th century. Let us add that, married to Ziba Nubar (daughter of Nubar Pasha), he had a daughter who became the Marques Genori and his granddaughter became princess Corsini.

It is interesting that the lineage of Nubar Pasha was no less distinguished. Through the women it is related to all the Gotha. There are links with the French nobility in the person of Count Philippe d'Arschot, Nubar's great-grandson, who married Rubis de Mun, whose mother was born Gontaut-Biron and the grand-mothers were respectively Princess de Bauffremont and Princess de Beauvau-Craon. Among other descendants of Nubar are Princess von Fürstenberg, Princess Windishgraetz, Princess Wolkonsky, Countess von Oppersdorf, etc...

The Balians

The Balian dynasty resided at Beshigtash, on the Bosphorus, and was very famous. Even those Turks who today deny the contribution of Armenians

* Quoted by Rouben Adalian.

to the Ottoman Empire tacitly recognize the importance of the Balians as imperial architects from the middle of the 18th century to the end of the 19th. For two centuries this family created the Ottoman splendour of Constantinople, covering it with magnificent buildings in a cultural encounter between East and West. From 1840 they were all trained in Paris at the Ecole des Beaux Arts. The family continuity of the Balians was one of the determining factors of their influence, whose starting point was the Era of the Tulips. Without compromising the architectural canons of the Orient or Islam, the Balians dominated a gradual westernization of official Ottoman architecture.

Their first known ancestor, Artin Bali, was established in Constantinople in 1682, where he died in 1725. He was probably a descendant of the Lords of Bali in Cilicia. He was appointed "Restorer of palaces and other buildings," a function to which his son Minas and grandson Magar succeeded, the latter as the builder of the Nouri-Osmaniye Mosque. Krikor Amira (1764–1831) was the son of Magar and the first illustrious Balian, appointed imperial architect by Sultan Abdul-Hamid I, and famous for his philanthropy. He regularly gathered together his masons for a Sunday banquet, which he gave in his large orchard at Baghlarbashi during which he liked to talk with each of them.

Krikor Amira also introduced Artin Kazaz to Mahmoud II. The latter, who disliked the baths installed by Krikor Amira in the imperial palace of Beshigtash, had him deported to Kayseri (Caesarea of Cappadocia) in 1821, until Artin Kazaz intervened. After a few months Artin Kazaz got some very good *pastirma*[*] which he knew the Sultan enjoyed greatly. He had a large piece wrapped in glazed paper and took it to the sovereign on behalf of his majesty's servant, Krikor Amira. "How is that, exclaimed the Sultan pretending to be astonished, Krikor Khalfa[†] is still in Caesarea? He must come back, I need his presence," and continuing in a low voice, while Kazaz kissed his hands, "The *pastirma* was used, till now, as bait on a mouse-trap; here it is promoted to the rank of a king-trap"...

Krikor Khalfa had so much influence on Mahmoud II that foreign ambassadors addressed him when submitting their requests to the Sultan who, in turn, also gave his reply through the same spokesman. The French

* An Armenian and Turkish cured meat speciality.

† *Khalfa* signifies architect in Turkish.

diplomats considered him as a "hyphen between the Seraglio and the (foreign) Powers."

The *yali* of Krikor Amira was situated on a hill overlooking Bulbuldere, which literally means, "valley of nightingales." This place got its name from the passion the Amira had for these birds, which he himself fed in his park. In his old age he spent hours seated listening to their song. It was wiser to indulge in the song of the nightingales than that of the muezzins...

Apart from the usual exemptions and prerogatives (fur coat, horse-riding, a beard...) Krikor Amira was allowed to move around on the Bosphorus in a caique with a double row of oarsmen.

His son and successor, Garabed Amira (1800–1866), continued the glory of the Balians. He is known for having visited, when a young man, the ruins of Ani, capital of mediaeval Armenia, and for being inspired by Armenian architecture in his own works. He was 31 when he was appointed imperial architect by Mahmoud II following Krikor Amira's death. He worked in a team, at first with his brother-in-law, Ohannes Amira Serverian, then with his elder son Nigoghos Bey, who was trained in France. His masterpiece is the palace of Dolma Bahche, finished in 1856.

During the three reigns of Mahmoud II, Abdul-Medjid and Abdul- Aziz, he maintained his reputation by adapting his style not only to the preferences of these Sultans, but also to the changing values of his time. In 1844 he was granted the privilege of wearing a fez bearing the imperial monogram.

During his career, lasting almost thirty years – the most productive part coinciding with the reign of Abdul-Medjid – he built seven palaces, four factories, a barracks, a mosque, two reservoirs and a tomb (that of Mahmoud II) and, for Armenians, seven churches, three schools, and two hospitals.

Garabed Khalfa was the last to bear the title of Amira. We have a portrait of him, the only one by an eye-witness, in this case a six years old child, so struck by the sight of the personality that it remained engraved in his memory for a long time, before being described forty-four years later in his "Monograph of the Magnate of Armenia."*

This description, which merits a complete translation, shows that the Amiras, even when they had lost their power, had not lost an inch of their pride. Here are the words of Artin Mirmirian:

> Garabed Amira Balian was given the titles of Chief of the Nation and Great Believer and was called the Khalfa.

---

* Published in 1910 by Artin Mirmirian.

> I was just six years old when, on hearing the ever-increasing murmur announcing the arrival of the Amira, I ran up the hill of Kouzkoundjouk-Idjadiye by which he would pass.
>
> That evening the Amira was riding a simply-harnessed horse which mounted the hill at a gentle trot. His inseparable servant Gaspard ran behind him. The passers-by came to a stand-still to salute him. Khalfa Amira, dominating his mount with his great stature, appeared to be 65 years old. On horseback he had a bearing resembling that of Krikor Effendi Karagheuzian,* but he was slimmer, more mature, more powerful and, above all, neater. He had an angular forehead half covered by a large fez, thick eyebrows, imposing and haughty, an abundant white moustache, pale and drooping cheeks and quite a large mouth. His long face, which expressed a deep but hidden self-content, conjured up a mixture of half-Asiatic, half-Byzantine nobility and command. His half-open lips and his piercing eyes were about to ask, loftily, "What's the matter?" to a beggar who had come to his feet and had to reply humbly to the question. The Amira wore a simple unironed hooded coat, a plain collar and a dark tie knotted around his sculptured neck. In his hand he held a slender cane which he used as a whip. Later on his manners were imitated by people who had amassed a large fortune but were never able to acquire a similar reputation or influence.

The eldest son of Garabed Amira, Nigoghos Bey Balian (1826–1858), studied at the College Sainte-Barbe. But before leaving for France, when he was still very young, he had to take part in a practical joke that the Sultan wanted to play on his father, Garabed. Mahmoud II sent for the child, made him sit in front of him – a position forbidden by protocol, legs crossed in addition! – and putting a hookah in his hand, invited him to smoke. Thereupon he summoned the father. One can easily imagine the panic that beset the unfortunate Amira on beholding this inconceivable spectacle. "What am I seeing, Nigoghos?" he stammered in Armenian, "What folly is this, lower your legs, you are going to ruin me, and what a posture!" and his voice choked while the Sultan laughed heartily. This anecdote shows the intimacy that could exist between Sultan and Amiras.

On his return from Sainte-Barde, Nigoghos became his father's assistant giving his own touch to the buildings that represented "the art of the

---

* A Banker.

Renaissance combined with European style and Ottoman taste," according to Pars Tuglaci, biographer of the Balians.

Fanatical in defending the rights of his masons, he endeavoured not only to improve their living conditions, he also set up with his own funds a school where European experts in the fields of technical construction, mural decoration and sculpture in relief taught his workers.

His innovations won him the affection of the gentle Sultan Abdul-Medjid who made him his artistic adviser. The superb mosque of Ortakeoy, elegant and slender, built in 1854–1855, can be considered the masterpiece of Nigoghos, who also designed the Dolma Bahche theatre which he completed shortly before he died in 1858.

His death, at the age of 32, greatly affected the Sultan, who ordered the Court to observe three days of mourning, which was unheard of for a Christian dignitary.

It should now be said that nothing is more fascinating than the minarets of Ottoman mosques, delicate columns soaring skywards, of a simple and elegant architecture, making them perhaps the purest masterpieces of Islamic art, more beautiful, no doubt, than the squat minarets of Egypt or Syria. In Cairo, for instance, the contrast is striking between the triumphant Ottoman mosque of Mehemet-Ali – built, they say, by an Armenian – and those no less glorious but more massive and less gracious in conception of the Fatimides and the Mameluks.

Once again, it is important not to forget that some of the most attractive minarets of Constantinople, marvels of Islamic art, were designed and sculpted by Christian hands immortalizing the name of the Balians.

The third son of Garabed Amira, Agop Bey Balian (1837–1875), also a graduate of the architectural department of the College Sainte-Barbe before continuing his studies in Vienna and Venice, returned to Constantinople on the death of his brother Nigoghos, to work with his father and his brother Sarkis. After the death of Garabed Amira (1866) he and his brother were appointed imperial architects and Agop Bey received the privilege of wearing a gold set-square and compass on his fez.

During his father's lifetime he drew up the plans of the Beylerbey Palace, completed by the two brothers in 1864. When the Empress Eugenie stayed there in 1869, she so admired it that she asked to see the two Balians to compliment and offer them gifts. She so appreciated the baths of the palace – a very modern conception even equipped with running water – that she

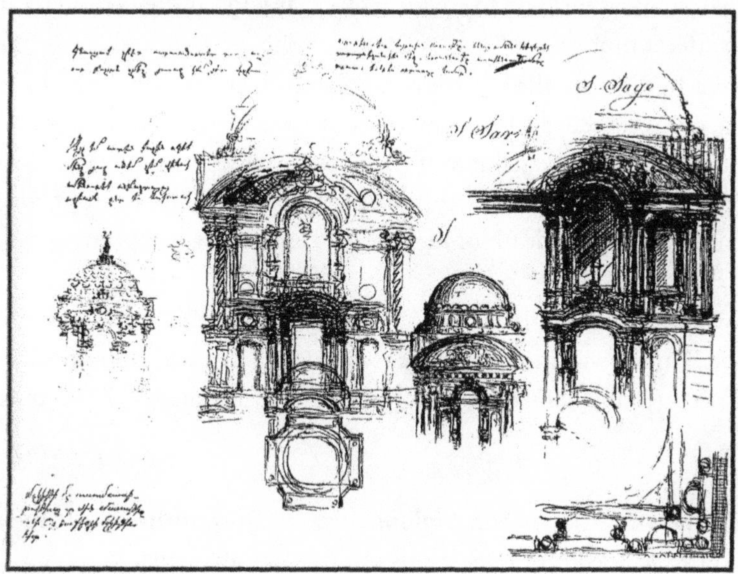

Sketch for a mosque by Agop Bey Balian

had a similar installation fitted at the Tuileries Palace. Agop Bey also built the Pavillon de Tokat for her.

He has left numerous plans and sketches of his buildings accompanied by commentaries in French and Armenian. Sultan Adbul-Aziz commissioned him to travel regularly to France to acquire the furniture and porcelain destined for Domla Bahche. One day he drew from memory, at the Sèvres porcelain factory, such a perfect copy of a soup tureen that it was given to him by the factory which kept the drawing in its archives.

Sarkis Bey (1831–1899), second son of Garabed Amira, was the last of the Balians to bear the title of Chief State Architect (*Ser Mimar-i-Devlet*).

Sarkis Bey had been a student not only at Saint-Barbe but at the Ecole Centrale and at the Beaux Arts. With his brother Agop, he built the palace of Beyerbey (1864) and then, alone, that of Yildiz (1876).

In 1874 Constantinople was struck by a severe earthquake which the edifices built by the Balians survived to the astonishment of Sultan Abdul-Aziz, who immediately promoted Sarkis Bey to the rank of Grand Officer of Osmania and the following year bestowed the Grand Cross of Medjidia.

The *Monde Illustré* wrote, in 1875, that Sarkis Bey built palaces and residences more quickly and at a lower cost than European architects. The magnificent palace of Beylerbey, which was the size of the Paris Opera, was built in only two years and the Yildiz Palace, as large as the National Library in Paris, in six months.

Simon Bey Balian, the fourth son of Garabed Amira, combined his talent as an accomplished architect with that of a skilful draughtsman and miniaturist. He was the painter of the frescoes which later covered the walls and ceilings of the palaces built not only by his father but also his grandfather. After the death of his brother Agop, he was appointed assistant imperial architect.

Leon Bey Balian, born in 1855, son of Nigoghos Bey, and grandson of Garabed Amira, was the last of the dynasty. He too had been a student at the Beaux Arts and assisted his uncle Sarkis Bey. He died in Paris in 1925.

The Dadians

The Dadians resided at San Stefano, on the Bosphorus. With them we touch on what was most prestigious in Ottoman Armenia.

Decendants of the Ardzrounis who reigned in Van in the Middle Ages, the Dadians established themselves in Constantinople with the banker Nigoghos Amira (1715–1763) whose son Arakel Dad Amira (1753–1812) was the first Dadian to bear the title of *Baroutdji Bashi* at the *Barouthane* (gunpowder factory), an essential institution of Ottoman armies. That was a paradoxical sight, for an Armenian to equip the Empire with firearms that Christians were forbidden to carry. Arakel Amira was also the initiator of the industrialization of Turkey.

We can do no better than quote Anahide Ter-Minassian to sum up, in a few lines, the action of the Dadians who, from 1795–1889, gave six *Baroutdji Bashi*s to the Empire:

> Directors of the Ottoman gunpowder factories since 1795, protected by Sultans Selim III and Mahmoud II, the Dadians played (…) a primordial role in the efforts to industrialize the State and in the creation around the capital and in Asia Minor of the first Imperial factories of gunpowder, firearms, paper, silk, cotton and cast iron. The most active, Ohannes Dadian, businessman, engineer and director, was a gifted inventor, on the look-out for technical innovations. From his study trips around Western Europe (1835, 1842, 1847) he brought back machines and English engineers. One of his sons built the first railway along the Bosphorus (1847). The Dadians also founded, at Zeytin Bournou, the first school of technical education which they ran and where they taught.

A most important event occurred in 1837. When visiting the firearms' factory that the Dadians managed at Dolma Bahche, Sultan Mahmoud II was so satisfied with the quality of those weapons that he addressed Ohannes Amira (1798–1869) with the ritual phrase whereby Ottoman Sultans declared their intention to reward one of their great servants: "Dile, benden ne dilersin?"* It was the first, but not the last time, that a Dadian was to be the object of such exceptional imperial favour. Ohannes Amira profited by the occasion to request the suppression of a particularly inhuman custom of giving Christian children to Turks as tribute. In its best known form, this tribute ensured the recruitment of Janissaries, abolished by Mahmoud II in 1826. But the practise continued to fulfil other tasks of which the Sultan appeared to be unaware. Furious, Mahmoud II immediately ordered the end of such cruelty. The credit of finally ending such a barbaric practice is thus due to the Dadians.

Ohannes Amira Dadian was raised to the rank of Bey by Sultan Abdul-Medjid after the publication of the Tanzimat (1840) proclaiming, in theory, equality between Christians and Muslims of the Empire. In fact, it was Mahmoud II, the father of Abdul-Medjid, who should have published the reforming decree. But he died before completing his policy. It was said of Mahmoud II, who supposedly had a Creole mother, Aimée du Bac de Rivery: "French blood flowed sufficiently in the veins of the Sultans to see them promise reforms, but not enough to apply them." These reforms were above all the work of the Grand-Vizier Reshid Pasha. Theoretical or not, they nonetheless aroused euphoria in the Empire, well summed up by a Greek: "If Reshid Pasha perseveres in his policy, we shall end up seeing the Turks fasting with us during Lent and us dining with them during Ramadan."

Let us return to Ohannes Bey. In 1856, at the end of the Crimean War, when France and England fought alongside the Turks against Russia, the weapons used in the Turkish ranks were produced by the Dadians' factories. The performance of these weapons led French officers to ask the *Baroutdji Bashi* the secrets of his weapons, promising the moon in exchange. Thus, a rash transaction was proposed to a man of honour and faith, who every morning assembled his family and servants to recite together a fervent *Hayr Mer* ("The Lord's Prayer" in Armenian) and was as much under obligation to the Sultan as he was a friend of France. In 1844 he had been received by

* "Ask, what do you ask of me?

Louis-Philippe. He belonged to the last generation of Amiras and to the first generation of the francophones of Armenian society of Constantinople. He was thus subject to three key influences: his own Armenian tradition, Turkish rule, and French culture. He represented a perfect example of this complex three-part world.

Of course Ohannes Bey cut short all negotiation with the French and refused to give up the secrets that belonged to the Ottoman Empire. The echo of his loyalty reached imperial ears. Abdul-Medjid immediately set off in his carriage, which he used for such expeditions, accompanied only by his coachman and a servant to avoid the company of the discontented members of his entourage who were hostile to Christians. When he arrived at San Stefano, where the Bey lived, the latter, who was informed at the last moment of his sovereign's arrival, was waiting on his doorstep. He made a large *temellah* to the great Sultan, a court greeting which consisted in touching the ground with the right hand and then the heart, lips and forehead, as a sign of submission and love. The sovereign then pronounced the famous phrase *"Dile, benden ne dilersin?"* "I wish long life to my Padishah," answered the Bey reverently. Indicating with a large gesture the site of San Stefano and the charm of its surroundings bristling with minarets and steeples, the sovereign said, "Ohannes Bey, all that you can see from where you stand and as far as the eye can see belongs to you and your descendants." Thus it was that the Dadians became the princes of San Stefano. The spectre was unheard of in Ottoman history, such were Armenian-Turkish relations at that time, but not for much longer.

This loyalty of Armenians was highly appreciated by the Turks, that is, the Great Turks. It was an era when they called Armenia the "faithful nation," *millet-i sadika.* Some of them even considered Armenians as "Christian Turks." Such an idea was, of course, false, since there was nothing in common between Armenians of Indo-European origin and Turks of Turanian origin belonging to the Ural-Altaic peoples.* However that may be, the idea of Christian Turks was apparently meant as a mark of respect.

One must admit, if one is not afraid to face the truth, that such examples, and many others of the same kind, illustrated the existence of real and unquestionable affinities between Armenians and Turks of that time.

* The history of these people, the forefathers of Finno-Ougrian and Turko-Mongol groups, starts in Central Asia. Later on, the Turks mixed with people from the Caucasus, especially Circassians and other beautiful Caucasian slaves.

The Russo-Turkish wars each time resulted in spectacular consequences for the Dadians. Twenty years after the Crimean War, the Russo-Turkish war of 1877–1878 led Russian troops to the gates of Constantinople. Sultan Abdul-Hamid entrusted Arakel Bey Dadian (1824–1912), the most prominent patrician of Ottoman and Apostolic Armenia, the task of greeting the Grand Duke Nicholas, brother of Tsar Alexander II, and Commander-in-Chief of the victorious armies, who had come to sign the peace of San Stefano – precisely at the fiefdom of the Dadians.

What were the reasons for this choice? Why did the Sultan not put a Turkish Pasha at the disposal of the Grand Duke? Why had he not entrusted the conqueror to the hospitality of a Greek dignitary of the Phanar – an Orthodox Christian like the Grand Duke? Perhaps he considered the Greeks too Russophile? But why choose an Armenian Prince when, on the Caucasian front, the Russian troops, commanded by the Russian-Armenian General Loris-Melikov, had just amputated the Turkish territory of two Armenian towns, Kars and Ardahan? The Sultan knew he could rely on the loyalty of the Dadians. He must have been fully aware that Arakel Bey would make it a point of honour to offer his imperial visitor the most sumptuous welcome, which would inevitably lead him, be it indirectly, to challenge the Turks for whom the Russians were the hereditary enemy.

Arakel Bey, quite naturally, rose up to the challenge. To enhance the quality of his welcome, he called upon his most brilliant relatives, who happened to be the three most prominent Armenians of the 19th century and lived beyond Turkish authority: one was Egyptian, the second Persian, and the third Russian.

The Egyptian was his brother-in-law, Nubar Pasha, of ancient Caucasian stock. We have already mentioned that he was the Egyptian Minister of Foreign Affairs and shortly Prime Minister. An exemplary reformer, unanimously respected by Europe, he was notably great friends with Disraeli and Bismarck who had the intention of placing him on the throne of Bulgaria – but a Russian veto wrecked this project in favour of the Prince of Battenberg.

The Persian was his son-in-law, Prince Mirza Malcolm Khan,* called the "regenerator of the Persian world," a remarkable diplomat, greatly appreciated by the Courts of London, Berlin and Rome, where he represented the Shah with rare elegance and talent. Anatole France offered

* See Chapters 4 & 5.

him one of his books with the following hand-written dedication: "To the prophetic spirit of Prince Malcom Khan as a token of friendship and admiration."

The Russian was his cousin, General Count Loris-Melikov, governor of Kharkov and conqueror of Kars, a notable man accompanying the Grand Duke. Tsar Alexander II was very soon to grant him full powers, in the midst of the nihilistic period, immortalized by the term "dictatorship of the heart."

Such were the three exceptional personalities, statesmen and nobles, whose presence at San Stefano, together with that of Arakel Bey, made the welcome given to the Grand Duke an extraordinary moment.

It should be added that all the ladies of the Dadian family were present, all renowned for their beauty, their intelligence, and their elegance.

When the Grand Duke entered the large drawing room of Arakel Bey's house and saw the brilliant assembly bathing in the light cast by silver candelabras two metres high, he stood still and said, "The Winter Palace is not more beautiful."

This event marked the climax of Ottoman Armenia, projecting into the limelight a lordly and supranational Armenia whose influence and alliances, ignoring frontiers, stretched over four monarchies and gave full significance to the hospitality offered by Arakel Bey to the Grand Duke Romanov, conqueror of Turkey.

It was the climax and also the swan song of Ottoman Armenia. Sultan Abdul-Hamid, already ill-inclined towards an Armenia whose credit, contrary to his predecessors, offended him, reacted with still greater resentment in the face of such a challenge.

Hadn't Armenia now fallen into a trap? Had he, who would become the "Red Sultan," not "magnified" Armenia to make her more suspect and vulnerable to future blows? From then on the irreparable policy slowly produced its effects, at first to restrain, then to destroy.

The office of *Baroutdji Bashi* was withdrawn from the Dadians by Abdul-Hamid in 1889, though this development did not result in the Dadians losing their title or prestige.

Before Abdul-Hamid acted so ruthlessly, the imperial visits made to the Princes of San Stefano were marks not only of satisfaction but also friendship.

In 1845, more than thirty years before receiving the Grand Duke, Arakel Bey had married an extraordinarily beautiful young woman who was called the "Lady Hamilton of Armenia" owing to the radiance of her beauty and humble birth.

The renown of this beauty went beyond the palace gates and came to the knowledge of Abdul-Medjid who dared what no other sultan had yet dared, since they did not consort with Christian women unless they were slaves. He summoned Boghos Bey Dadian (1802–1863), who was Arakel's father, and asked to see his daughter-in-law. Taken aback, the *Baroutdji Bashi* did not show his surprise but hurried to inform his son of the imperial request. This created great consternation amongst the Dadians, each member hesitating between the audaciousness of the request and the rank of the asker who, at that time, only saw women, other than those of the harem, either veiled or not at all. However, as was to be expected, the objections were passed over in silence owing to the idea of the honour, unusual as it was, shown to the Dadians, who were known to be very keen on their social advancement.

Aroused by the idea of a feminine encounter, certainly platonic but nonetheless exciting, Abdul-Medjid returned to San Stefano where he was greeted on alighting from his carriage by the double *temellah* of both father and son bowing down to the ground. Then he entered the pretty residence which he knew well and was served raki. Madame Arakel Bey appeared and curtseyed in French style to the sovereign. Captivated, Abdul-Medjid forgot to drink his raki. He gazed for a long time in silence at the superb creature standing in front of him, radiant with a grace of a goddess. He murmured several times, "What beauty, Lord, what beauty." Then, turning towards Arakel, he said in a very Turkish fashion, "*Oghloum*,* take good care of your wife. You have shown her to me because I asked you, but do not show her to anyone else."

Then the Dadians, as if wishing to alternate the profane and the sacred, and drown the beauty of the woman in the smiles of angels, sent for the choir of the nearby Armenian church to sing for the Caliph some of the most beautiful psalms of Armenian liturgy. How symbolic! It is worth noting that, of all the Amiras, the Dadians were the greatest builders of churches. They built some not only on their own lands but also at Eyoub, Haskeoy, Nicomedia, Armash, Brousse, etc...

---

* Oghloum (*Ott. Tr.*): My son.

In 1858, Ohannes Bey (1834–1919), younger brother of Arakel, married Takouhi Karakehia, sister of Abraham Pasha and sister-in-law of Nubar Pasha. With his fine features and her black eyes, he a cultivated man and she an intelligent woman, this attractive couple lived in Paris in their town house on Avenue Gabriel. Ohannes Bey was, amongst other things, a numismatist and possessed a remarkable collection of French medals. He and his wife gave the impression of being accomplished aristocrats, extremely kind and benevolent; they were nicknamed "Philemon and Bauci" as they were so united.

Here is a pretty anecdote dating from the adolescence of Ohannes Bey, as related by his granddaughter Anna Boutros Ghali. In 1847, Ohannes and one of his brothers, at the time boarders at the College Sainte-Barbe, accompanied the Turkish Ambassador and two imperial princes to Paris. One evening, when they were invited to the royal box at the Opera, the appearance of all these young boys with their tarbouches and long tassels (those of the princes decorated with diamond crescents) so charmed the public that they were applauded at great length.

The third brother of Arakel Bey, Mardig Bey (1836–1914), was very different. He also made a brilliant match in 1860 by marrying Malvina de Savallan, the daughter of an old Armenian family from Persia, established for over a century in Smyrna. She was also of incomparable beauty, but aggressive and ravaging. She was dubbed "the black rose." Terrified at the idea of taking her for a wife, Mardig Bey fled at the moment of the nuptial blessing and hid himself in a hen house from where he had to be pulled out and, covered in feathers, brought back to the altar. Such behaviour was all the more inappropriate since Mardig's sister Nounia Dadian was marrying the Russian-Armenian Prince Argoutinsky at the same time in the same church. The French Ambassador, Bourrèe, who attended the double ceremony, recalls in his memoirs the splendour of the marriage rather than the feathers of the bridegroom! Mardig and Malvinia made an eccentric couple. He often had absurd ideas. One day he thought he was misunderstood and forgotten by all and decided to organize his own funeral in order to determine the degree of indifference he felt from others. To his surprise and joy, a crowd of friends thronged at his "funeral," where he made a theatrical appearance declaring, "Thank you, my dearly beloveds for coming in such numbers to show your sympathy for him who is so happy to still be in your midst." After his real death, his widow, weeping less for the loss of her husband than that of her beauty, closed the door on her admirers, going even so far as to refuse to receive the men of the family. The couple's son, Boghos, was so captivated by the divine bottle that if a match was lit near his lips, they would catch fire. His sister Marie married the Georgian Prince Vassili Gouriel.

The eccentricities of the Dadians had no limit. During lent, the members of this family did not fast but gave up smoking and wore black gloves. Madame de Hubsch, a Belgian who cut a figure in Istanbul society, said to the Dadians: "You are eccentrics and I adore you, but you are eccentrics nonetheless."

Like others, the Dadians were not spared by the quarrels between Catholic and Apostolic Armenians, each calling on Turks to arbitrate! In 1863, Boghos Bey Dadian was entrusted by Sultan Abdul-Aziz to carry out a mission in France whose nature we do not know. On arrival in Paris he fell ill and died. In the absence of Apostolic monks – the Armenian church in Paris was only founded thirty years later – he was given his final rites by an Armenian Catholic priest who asserted that, before dying, Boghos Bey converted to the Roman faith, an assertion that the family of the deceased did not accept.

At the landing stage of Constantinople the two Patriarchs, Catholic and Apostolic, resolutely awaited the mortal remains of Boghos Bey Dadian, each wishing to take possession thereof. To avoid a scandal, they both decided to have recourse to Turkish mediation and the arbitration of the Grand-Vizier, Fouad Pasha. "Beatitude," said the Grand-Vizier after careful consideration and addressing the Catholic prelate, "you certify that you are in possession of the soul of the deceased?" "Yes, indeed Excellency," replied his interlocutor. "In that case, you can leave the body to the Armenians," settled the skilful Pasha in a gentle voice, who obviously did not wish to displease the Dadians. Does not this example illustrate the famous wisdom attributed to the Orient? The funeral of Boghos Bey was grandiose. It was a measure of the great prestige of the Dadians. Planned to the smallest detail, the funeral cortege was organized as follows:

> Two guards lead the cortege, each carrying a candle,
> hands not gloved;
> The fanfare, sent by the Sublime Porte;
> Twenty guards each carrying a candle, hands not gloved;
> Eight door-keepers of the Pera Commission, empty handed;

Ten ushers of the Palace, empty handed;
A cross-bearer and two crozier-bearers, gloved hands;
Thirty altar-boys each carrying a candle, wearing white gloves,
Candles draped in black;
Ten deacons, identical presentation;
Some "kahanas" (married parish priests) without a chasuble, carrying a candle;
Some "vartabeds" (learned priests), two by two, wearing a chasuble and carrying a candle;
The "Suisse" of the Patriarch carrying his large candle and accompanied on each side by two tall kahanas without candles;
Some bishops wearing a chasuble and holding their cross;
The Patriarch wearing a chasuble, carrying his crozier and cross, accompanied by two young altar-boys each holding the
edge of the chasuble;
The coffin carried on the shoulders of four beadles dressed in black and wearing a fez;
One on each side of the coffin, four torches carried by Armenian civil servants in uniform with black mourning-band;
The six cordons of the pall held by Amiras.

Can one imagine a more spectacular tribute? The Osmanli Empire sending a detachment of the imperial guard to honour a Christian funeral?

In 1907 a great-granddaughter of Boghos Bey, Anna Aslan, married Naguib Bey Boutros-Ghali, son of the Prime Minister of Egypt, Boutros Pasha Ghali (assassinated in 1910). In her memoirs* she writes: "When I came to Egypt, the son-in-law of the Turkish High Commissioner, on a visit to Boutros Pasha, having heard that his daughter-in-law was from Constantinople, asked to see me. I was presented to him and, as it became an elderly man or perhaps to avoid my father-in-law from getting up, he remained seated and said to me: 'What is your family?' I answered 'I am from the *Baroutdji Bashi.*' He then stood up and said 'it is our most noble family.' My father-in-law smiled and seemed satisfied."

The sixth and last *Baroutdji Bashi*, Simon Bey Dadian (1829–1899) resigned his functions nobly when Abdul-Hamid II decided to exclude

* A. N. Boutros-Ghali, *Les Dadians, Souvenirs de famille*, Cairo (undated, written around 1965).

Armenian workers from the imperial gunpowder factories. But the title of *Baroutdji Bashi* remained attached only to the Dadian family. Several years after the fall of Abdul-Hamid II (1909), his successor, Mehmed V, asked, "Why do the *Baroutdji Bashi* no longer come to see me?" Ohannes Bey left this appeal unanswered. He wished to keep his distance to the Palace owing to the terrible massacres in the provinces.

The Duz

The Duz resided at Kuru Cheshme ("Dry Fountain" in Turkish) on the Bosphorus. They belonged to the most illustrious family of Catholic Armenia.

The first known ancestor of this family is only identified by his forename: Artin. In 1600 he settled in Constantinople where, as a talented artist, he became goldsmith to the Palace. His son, Sarkis (who died in 1721), succeeded him. He was the first to bear the name Duz, whose origin is subject to several interpretations. According to one of them, the Sultana Validé ordered a ring which was so perfect that she said to him, "Ask me what you wish. I will grant it to you." When the goldsmith replied that he asked for no more than the agreed price, the Sultana said, "I have rarely met a man as *duz* (honest) as you..." According to another version, Sultan Ahmed III – responsible for the "Tulip Era" – noticing the aforementioned Sarkis in the park of the Palace, was struck by his tall stature and said to his entourage, "Send for this *duz*," and thus the name remained.

Sarkis had a son and successor Ohannes Duz (who died in 1744). He served as Imperial Goldsmith under Sultan Mahmoud I, with whom he was a close acquaintance. Michael Chelebi* (1724–1783) was the son of Ohannes and the most famous of the Duz. He succeeded his father after learning drawing and chemistry, as well as the goldsmith's trade, in which he surpassed all his predecessors. In 1758 he was appointed director of the Mint (in Turkish *Darbhane*, that is to say, "house where coins are struck"), an important position for a Christian, until then occupied by Jews, the last being Yako Bonfil. For a long time powerful and prosperous, the Jews had

* Chelebi (*Ott. Tr.*): Prince, a title given to the Duz Amiras.

fallen into decline and Yako Bonfil had fallen into disgrace. Sultan Mustapha III went as far as banning them, threatening to ostracise those of his successors who might be tempted to give them back the *Darbhane*. For many years the victims of these measures tried to recover their lost positions.

Michael Chelebi was as well known for his generosity as well as his honesty. During the Greek uprising in 1769, following the Russo-Turkish war of 1768–1774, he intervened to save thousands of Greeks from Ottoman revenge. Later on, in a sale of ancient objects of the Palace, he acquired a sword in copper which, on closer examination, he discovered to be gold. He cleaned it, restored its lustre, and gave it back to the Treasury. This gesture won him the full confidence of Sultan Mustapha III. Michael Chelebi died on August 13th 1783 of an attack of apoplexy.

Michael Chelebi's eldest son, Ohannes (1749–1812), who was also one of the family celebrities, succeeded him as head of the Imperial Mint and director of the Imperial Goldsmiths. His lively intelligence, prudence and loyalty pleased Sultan Selim III, who also enjoyed the serenades on the lyre and cithara by Ohannes' brother and sons. The latter, who had the monopoly of the Ottoman silk industry, entrusted its management, in 1802, to the future Artin Amira Kazaz who, being very experienced in the weaving of silks, carried out the task to the full satisfaction of his master. In 1807 Kazaz heard that an officer of the Janissaries, Hadji Mustapha Kazandji, was preparing to kill Sultan Selim III and several dignitaries, as well as four prominent members of the minorities: a Greek, a Jew and two Armenians, one being none other than Ohannes Duz. Ohannes Kazaz ran to see this officer and, by dint of entreaties and bribes, succeeded in cancelling his gruesome project. The future Amira thus began a long series of difficult endeavours, each time crowned with success, making him a providential man.

In 1811, Ohannes Chelebi, a Catholic, had the honour of pleading for the rights of Apostolic Armenians concerning the Patriarchate of Jerusalem; rights contested once more by the Greeks who had "bought" the Grand-Vizier Keor Youssouf Pasha, who was depicted as a "wicked, greedy man." To face this situation, the Amiras formed a "national unity," in other words, an unusual union between Catholic and Apostolic Armenians, for a national cause supported by Ohannes Duz. Fortunately for Armenia, war broke out between Turkey and Russia and Keor Youssouf Pasha took command of operations. To replace him, a deputy Vizier was nominated whom the

Amiras hurried to win over with the help of Ohannes Chelebi. At that time, the influential Garabed Amira Aznavorian (1745–1853) was at their head as Chief Banker of the Empire and held the very coveted title of *mutevelli*, attributed by the Patriarch, giving him a priority say in the affairs of the Church and Nation. In this way the Jerusalem Patriarchate was saved with the consent of the Sultan. Ohannes Chelebi died the following year, on April 9th 1812.

To ensure his succession, an unusual procedure was adopted. The Imperial Mint fell to the eldest son of the deceased, Krikor Chelebi (1774–1819) and the Imperial Goldsmith fell to the second son, Sarkis Chelebi (1777–1819). Why this separation? Did this measure conceal a failing, a reduction in influence? If the direction of the Mint was considered more honourable, the Imperial Goldsmith focused on itself the reality of power. It controlled, notably, throughout Europe and Asia, the commerce not only of gold but of precious stones and above all pearls, which Jean-Pierre Peroncel-Hugoz rightly calls the "oil" of the time.*

Garabed Amira Aznavorian (1745–1853)

The honesty of the Duz was not involved. The sons had their father's competence but they lacked his caution. They lived on a grand scale, wore expensive clothes which, as we know, did not go unnoticed in the Turkey of that time. As Father Menevichian, their biographer wrote, Krikor, the elder, "had an exaggerated propensity for magnificence and for ostentatious luxury."† The two brothers, moreover, had a sumptuous yali built at Yenikeoy, on the Bosphorus.

The prestige of the Duz was such that it was impossible to dismiss them from their posts, all the more because they had the entire favour of the

* See "The Beautiful Orient of Exotic Pearls" in *Le Monde* (May 17th 1996).

† Menevichian, Gabriel *Azkapanoutioun Aznouvagan Zarmin Duziantz* [Genealogy of the Noble Duz Family], Vienna, 1890.

Sultan. Thus it is that Mahmoud II had given a personal contribution of 30,000 piastres towards the building of their residence at Yenikeoy. But this luxury and favour inevitably resulted in the alliance of numerous enemies against the Duz. Two of them plotted their downfall: one was Turkish, the other Jewish. The more formidable was the Turk called Haled Effendi, former ambassador to Paris under Napoleon I. He had become the favourite of Mahmoud II, whom he manipulated at will. Enemy of the Christians, he was particularly against the Duz from whom he had borrowed large sums of money before taking up his post at the Paris Embassy... He believed that the best way of being quit of his debts was to get rid of his creditors!

As for the Jew, called Isrel, he was the Turk's banker and appreciated his position in the hope of getting the Imperial Mint back in Jewish hands, and in his hands in particular. Acting through an intermediary and without warning, Haled ordered, on August 29th 1819, the inspection of the accounts of the *Darbhane*. A few overdrafts were brought to light, the most important being that granted to Haled himself, something Haled never mentioned – the Duz, as men of honour, having left no trace of his name in their books.

The other discoveries concerned usual dealings which were nonetheless held against them. On that same day the two Duz brothers were confined to the Mint and then, on September 19th, transferred to a sordid prison where they were incarcerated with all the men of their family, as well as their employees and their servants. As for their wives, they were confined in the Patriarchate. In all, about forty people of both sexes were thrown into prison.

But the Sultan was still not entirely convinced of the culpability of the Duz. However, his attitude towards them was overturned by an unexpected event. Seals were placed on the residence of the Duz, first on their palace at Kourou Cheshme. A thorough search revealed the existence of a secret Catholic chapel. The Turks, we know, were aware of the sympathy of some Armenians to Rome, but such clear appurtenance to a foreign religion, forbidden to the subjects of the Sultan, appeared a crime of *lèse-majesté* and paradoxically weighed more heavily than the alleged dilapidation of the Treasury. Thus it was that Mahmoud II abandoned the Duz whom he had so loved, to their inevitable fate.

The conspirators had a free hand to apply capital punishment that they had plotted long before. On October 4th 1819, Krikor and Sarkis Duz were beheaded in the presence of the Sublime Porte while their younger brother Mikael and their cousin Megerdich were hung at a window in their palace of Yenikeoy. The arbitrary procedure and the horror of these measures plunged Ottoman Armenia and Christian Constantinople, including the Ambassadors, into shock and consternation. According to Turkish custom, the bodies of the four Duz, who had been executed, should have been thrown into the sea. To save them from such a fate, Matheos Amira Allahverdi, banker to the Grand-Vizier, secretly handed him the sum of 2,500 gold pounds to buy the bodies of those executed. The bodies were taken by boat, at night, to Kourou Cheshme, where they received a secret but decent burial in their family cemetery.

The minister of the Navy, Abdullah Pasha, who knew the Duz to be innocent, requested from the Sultan that the lives of the three youngest brothers of the condemned – Hagop, Garabed and Boghos – be spared. They were sent to an Armenian monastery in Caesarea where they lived in obscurity for three years.

Isrel thought that the moment had come to seize the Mint with Haled's help like a ripe fruit. But this turned out to be a forbidden fruit. The Sheikh-ul-Islam soon reminded the Sultan of the 1758 ban: no Jew at the head of the *Darbhane.* While Isrel consoled himself by seizing the palace of the Duz at Kourou Cheshme, Mahmoud II maintained the Mint in Armenian hands. He temporarily entrusted it, with the title of Amira, to Artin Kazaz, who had long been a close acquaintance of the *Darbhane.* Then two Armenian Catholics succeeded in turn at the head of the Mint, which returned to Kazaz from 1827 to 1834.

The affair of the secret chapel had tumultuous effects. The possessions of the Duz, which were considerable, in particular in their palace of Kourou Cheshme, were auctioned in May and June 1820. They attracted many people, including some Amiras. Isrel, the new master of the place, was of course present. On the first day of the sale, approaching the chapel, he seized the ciborium and pronounced the word "*tükürdanlik.*"* He had scarcely uttered the blasphemy when he was knocked over by a slap in the face from Ohannes Amira Yerganian. The latter immediately saw his death sentence in the hateful look cast by the man at his feet. Realizing that his only hope of salvation was through abjuration, the Amira quickly embraced Islam and was the only one of his class to have ever made such a conversion.

From then on he was safe and all paths were open to him: he asked for, and obtained, the direction of the customs of the Empire. He knew what he

* Tükürdanlik (*Ott. Tur.*): Spittoon.

was up to. He suspected that the real culprits were not the Duz, but rather the new favourite of the Sultan and his banker. He hoped that his new duties would enable him to unmask them. Meanwhile he had to comply to the constraints of his conversion. He had to leave his wife and children and, according to Islamic law, take a Muslim wife. Every week a woman – we don't know who – came to see him in secret to give news of his family whom he never saw again.

After a year of relentless search, he attained his ends: the control of the customs enabled him to intercept suitcases full of false gold coins stamped with the monogram of Mahmoud II and intended for the two felons, whom he handed over to the justice of the Sultan. After that episode no more was ever heard of him. The conspirators were beheaded in their turn, whereas, on the intercession of Artin Amira Kazaz, the surviving Duz returned to Constantinople where they recovered their belongings and, in particular, their palace of Kourou Cheshme.

One cannot help to wonder why these Duz, whom Turkey had so harmed, returned to Constantinople and gave to the Empire three more directors of the Mint, whereas they could easily have turned their backs on the Empire and lived comfortably in Europe. All the paradox of the Ottoman Empire resided in this dilemma, being torn between attraction and horror.

This dilemma, impossible to solve, is personified in Mihran Bey Duz (1817–1891), son of Sarkis Chelebi, who was just two years old at the time of his father's death. Many years later, Mihran carried out the same functions as his father, except that – due to fashion – he abandoned the imposing headgear and great coat edged with sable or ermine for the fez and the uniform studded in gold and decorations of Ottoman top civil servants. The latter had been metamorphosed as "Westerners" by the reforms of 1840.

The last descendant of the Duz was Sarkis Bey Duz, who was born in Constantinople in 1889 and died in Paris in 1982. While writing these lines one can recall the features of this very distinguished octogenarian, seated in the company of Hermine Aslan under the imposing portraits of his grandfather Mihran Bey in uniform and his great-grandfather Sarkis Chelebi wearing the monumental *kalpak* of the Amiras and decapitated in 1819.

M. and Mme. Mihran Bey Duz (1817-1891)

The affair of the secret chapel of the Duz was, as we have already mentioned, accepted very badly by the Turks. The Grand-Vizier summoned the Patriarch and asked him to put an end once and for all to the Roman obedience of Armenian Catholics. This affair triggered a severe crisis. Frightened, and rightly so, by the fate reserved for the Duz, the Catholic Amiras said they were ready to make concessions to the Apostolic Church whose protectors – the Dadians and the Balians for a start – showed similar disposition towards Catholics. It was evidently not a question of submitting to Rome but of establishing with the Vatican, at the cost of relatively minor mutual concessions, a *modus vivendi* in order to allay the anger of the Turks. But these arrangements led to nothing tangible. The year 1820 was marked throughout by a succession of rapprochements followed by retractions, such sterile moves that it would be useless to enter into their details. Why say "throughout the year" when one should say "a whole century"?!

In this context, let us briefly touch on the very controversial Mgr. Hassoun, Patriarch of Catholic Armenia, who, during much of the 19th century sowed discord not only between Catholic and Apostolic Armenians in Turkey, but between the Catholics themselves. The latter became divided between hassounists and anti-hassounists, the quarrel ending only in 1888, when Edgar Bey Duz, representing the moderate wing (anti-Hassounists) married Nectar Allahverdi, representative of the radical wing (Hassounists). The Armenians of both sides ended up obtaining the recall of Mgr. Hassoun to Rome, where, in exchange, Pope Leon XIII made him a cardinal, the first Armenian, well before Mgr. Agajanian who almost became Pope in 1958.

However, the important moment in attempts to unite Apostolic and Catholic Armenians was in 1845 when Rome sent Cardinal Ferrieri to Constantinople in the hope of smoothing out the disagreements of a denominational nature which embittered Armenia. Alternating at first with amiable words and then less amiable remarks, the Cardinal ended by condemning all Greeks and Armenians as being guilty of schism. Matheos Patriarch of Armenia took it very badly and wanted to inform the Sublime Porte, but Ohannes Amira Dadian and Garabed Amira Balian, still hoping to come to an understanding with Rome, vetoed this move. Worried, Matheos Patriarch went to see his Greek counterpart to open his heart and tell him that he wished to see the departure of the Catholic Prince of the Church. "I am aware of everything," replied the Oecumenical Patriarch, "and I shall inform the Porte at once."

The head of the Greek Church explained to the head of the Turkish Government that the remarks made by Cardinal Ferrieri created trouble within the Christian communities of the Empire. The Grand-Vizier, using traditional channels, intervened with the French Ambassador to let him know that the presence of the Roman messenger had become undesirable in Turkey. The Ambassador immediately took the necessary steps to remove the Cardinal, who complied immediately with the orders of the trustee of the Capitulations.

The Noradounghians

The Noradounghians resided on the heights of Cheragan from where they dominated the Bosphorus.

As *Ekmekdji Bashi,* "Head Breadmaker" of the Empire, Artin Amira Noradounghian (1770–1843) ensured, on a massive scale, the daily supply of bread to the Sultan and his Court. Like most of his peers, this Amira also lived on a grand scale. He owned a large *konak* overlooking the Bosphorus, surrounded by a still larger park planted with roses which perfumed the air with their fragrance and pleased the eye with their beauty. Indoors, the walls were covered with murals and the ceilings were decorated with superb woodwork, all being of great value. Moreover, a library, no doubt the largest in Constantinople, contained no less than five thousand books, a third of which were in Armenian, the rest in French.

A man of taste and culture, Artin Amira was also, like his peers, an authoritarian who liked to be obeyed, especially by the clergy. One day, he demanded the resignation of the Patriarch, Asdvadzadour II, who had only reigned three years (1841–1844) and had nothing to blame himself for. One day, as the Amira became more pressing, the prelate said, while scribbling some words on a piece of paper, "Come, Amira, that I may give you this note," which, after folding and sealing, he handed to the Amira. The Patriarch instructed him to take it personally to the Grand-Vizier. On opening it, the latter did not read an act of resignation by the Patriarch but the order to exile the Amira, who put up a brave face. Let us wager that the Sultan, not able to do without his daily bread, stopped the exile of his Head Breadmaker. But this anecdote shows that, however submissive they may have been to the Amiras, the Patriarchs knew, when necessary, how to embarrass them. Asdvadzadour Patriarch was far from regretting the occasion which had enabled him to have his say.

Gabriel Noradounghian (1852–1941)

The grandson of Artin Amira was none other than the great Gabriel Effendi Noradounghian, who was the best legal expert of the Empire. He worked for the Ottoman Ministry of Foreign Affairs at a time when the descendants of the Amiras had ceased to be bankers. Gabriel Effendi received the portfolio of Foreign Affairs at the time of the Balkan Wars (1912–1913).

Let us add, as a note of history, that only five years after Gabriel Effendi became Ottoman Minister of Foreign Affairs, his son, Diran, became Armenia's ambassador to the Vatican. Further mention will be made of the "Brief Armenia" that existed from 1918 to 1920. But was it not astonishing to see, in such a short space of time, the father heading Ottoman diplomacy and the son representing the Republic of Armenia?

Just another word about this Ambassador who kept his embassy barely two years. After World War II, Madame Artin Effendi Aslan gathered the last aristocrats of Ottoman Armenia for tea in Paris. The first to arrive was Diran Bey Noradounghian, who was very moved to find himself among the Aslans. He told them that sixty years earlier he had received a toy from Artin Effendi and had been very fond of it. Sarkis Bey Duz was announced. As more and more came, Diran Bey rose saying, "One would think we were in Constantinople!" It was the *cri du coeur*. Constantinople, always Constantinople! Ohannes Bey Gulbenkian arrived, a descendant of Arakel Bey Dadian through the female line, of which he was very proud. After a remark or a gesture, Madame Artin Effendi, who could have been his mother, said to him, *"Ohannes, Dadian esse, Dadian!"*[*] Ohannes was unable to contain his outburst of joy. "*Hanoum*" he said, falling to his knees, "*Tserkernit hampourem.*"[†] Such was the atmosphere, theatrical and unreal, in which these people were immersed.

It was just below the *konak* of the Noradounghians that the Balians had built the very beautiful Imperial Palace of Cheragan. At the end of the 19th century, in 1896, following an armed incident when Armenian revolutionaries took over the Ottoman bank for one day, it was decided that the residence of the Norodounghians, situated on a hill that unfortunately overlooked the Palace of Cheragan, could not be left in non-Turkish hands, especially in Armenian hands, even though the Noradounghians had nothing in common with the revolutionaries.

The descendants of Artin Amira resigned to the sale of the *konak* for a song to an ignorant Turkish Pasha – a complete fool, it was said – who wrought havoc in the rosebeds and the woodwork with pickaxes. Although lacking in culture, the Turk soon realized that the upkeep of such a house was beyond his means. He sold it to another Turk. The latter took advantage of the fire that had destroyed the splendid Palace of Cheragan and stated that the place was no longer a strategic one. He was thus able to sell it to "non-Turks," in this case to the Jewish community of Constantinople, who turned it into an orphanage. However, as the transaction turned out to be unprofitable, the Israelites had the place demolished in 1946 and built in its place – house and park included – twenty modern properties to rent.

---

* "Ohannes, say Dadian, Dadian!"

† "Madame, I kiss your hands."

Two Portraits at the Juncture of a Century

Artin Amira Kazaz (1771–1834)

We have already mentioned the name of Artin Amira Kazaz, the most popular of the Amiras, who knew how to formulate artful stratagems to resolve the most difficult problems. He had the gift of intervening to rescue all and sundry from hazardous situations. We have already mentioned the spectacular episode of the belfry of the church of Haskeoy.

In 1821 Kazaz became the personal banker of Mahmoud II and the following year replaced the wretched Haled in the Sultan's favour. Kazaz Amira, contrary to most of his peers, was neither Agntsi nor an aristocrat; he was the son of a modest draper. He belonged to that category of men who demand respect: starting with nothing, he had neither the vulgarity of an upstart nor the arrogance of the social climber. He was an intelligent, authentic, self-made man who became a gentleman. For twelve years he was the person who had the ear of Sultan Mahmoud II. According to legend, the latter, one night, when feeling very dispirited, gave Kazaz the insignia of imperial power enabling him to govern the Empire in his place. The Turks were furious and the Europeans resentful at seeing the Sultan bewitched to such a degree by the ever-present Armenian. Artin Amira was, behind the scenes, the instigator and organizer of the massacre of the Janissaries who had deposed and killed the eight predecessors of Mahmoud II. They had formed a State within the State, and after terrorizing the enemies of Turkey, they had turned on the Turks who were only set free from such a scourge by the massacre that took place in 1826.

Seven years after the bloody events, the Russian armies stationed at Constantinople were mobilised to rescue Mahmoud II, driven with his back to the wall by the invasion of his vassal Mehemet Ali, viceroy of Egypt. The sultan had said at the time, "A drowning man clings to a snake,"* and had appealed to the Tsar, to the *Moskof*, the hereditary enemy of the Turks. Russia saved Turkey but demanded in exchange the payment of a colossal tribute which, had it not been paid, would have made the Ottoman Empire into a Russian province (at least temporarily, because other European

---

* A Kurdish proverb.

powers would never have accepted such a development). The Treasury was empty and the sovereign dismayed. He sent for Kazaz and asked him what should be done. "Leave it to me, Padishah," replied Kazaz who, in three days, managed to collect the required sum and brought it to the Padishah. Mahmoud II was unable to believe his eyes. He stood up and removed the chain of the Order of the Imperial Effigy that he was wearing, *Tasvir-i-Humayoun*, the highest distinction of the Empire, and placed it round Kazaz's neck. That was a supreme honour, something unbelievable, which no other Armenian, Christian or Jew had yet received nor was to receive later. When Kazaz took leave of the sultan, all the Turks who saw him thus adorned prostrated themselves in front of him. Armenia had never been so intimately involved in Ottoman politics.

But after all that, Kazaz never neglected Armenia's interests and those of its Church. In 1832, for instance, without consulting Kazaz, Mahmoud II gave his consent to certain men who sought, arbitrarily, to remit to the Treasury the revenues of the Greek and Armenian churches and monasteries. These two minorities were greatly alarmed but knew that they could only rely on Kazaz to have this unjust decree revoked. This powerful Amira went to the Palace carrying an empty oil lamp and stood still staring at his lamp near the Sultan's room. Seeing the strange sight Mahmoud II asked, "What have you got in your hand?" "Oh Padishah," replied the Amira, mixing Islam and Christianity as in the case of the Haskeoy church, "Jesus and his Holy Mother Mary having no oil to burn in their churches have sent the lamp to your Highness." Immediately grasping the allusion, the Sultan ordered that the administration of their revenues be given back to the Christian minorities. One could multiple such examples.

On the death of Kazaz, Hagop Chelebi Duz, one of the brothers of the condemned Duz, removed the insignia of the Order of the Imperial Effigy from the breast of the deceased and gave it back to the Sultan who, on seeing it, was unable to suppress his emotion. It is said that he attended Kazaz' funeral disguised as a peasant or a monk. Let us retain rather the version according to which the naval ships escorting the caïque carrying the body from his abode to the Patriarchate at Kum Kapu made a detour in order to pass by the Imperial Palace where Mahmoud II, from the balcony, said a last farewell to his long time counsellor and confidant. As for the Patriarch, he had already bestowed on Artin Amira Kazaz the title, unique in its kind,

"Unrivalled Benefactor of the Nation" (*Azkayin Anzoukagan Parerar* in Armenian).

Artin Amira Kazaz (1771–1834)

Let us digress for a moment. It was mentioned that the Russians almost annexed the Ottoman Empire. Before that, in 1828, they conquered a large part of Persian Armenia, including Echmiadzin and Yerevan, leaving Iran only the small territory bordered on the east by Lake Ourmiah. Around a hundred thousand Apostolic Armenians living in the eastern provinces of Ottoman Turkey then emigrated to Russia. In 1831, France negotiated with the Sublime Porte for the creation of an autonomous Patriarchate responsible for Catholic Armenians who were thereafter considered to belong to the "Catholic Nation"…

Thus Armenia was situated at the cross-roads of great international political and religious developments which soon bore heavily on her own existence.

Megerditch Amira Djezahirli (1805–1861)

Belonging to one of the great families of Haskeoy, Megerdich Amira Djezahirli was the modernist of his time. As such he was the *bête noire* of his extremely conservative peers and was seen as a challenger.*

When the fashion in Turkey conformed to strict rules he decided to ignore them and dress in European style. In a gesture of supreme bravado, while the Sultan still lived in wooden palaces, Megerdich Amira had a palace built in stone. He was called "The Fouquet of Armenia"!

Better still. In order to link an industrialized zone of Constantinople with his town of Haskeoy, which was to be the main beneficiary, the Amira had a monumental bridge built which he inaugurated by mounting his superb steed and prancing all alone on the bridge. In doing so, he flouted

* This Amira got his name from his grandfather, Ohannes Amira Djezahirli, who, at the end of the 18th century, had been banker and guarantor of the Ottoman governors of Algeria (*Djezahir* in Turkish).

the rule whereby only the Sultan had the right to inaugurate such an important structure. His enemies did not fail to inform the gentle Abdul-Medjid, who was annoyed by such daring and sent for the proud patrician for an explanation. "Oh Padishah, I only wanted to test the solidity of the bridge before seeing your Highness cross over…" was the reply. The bridge was nonetheless destroyed by the adversaries of the Amira after his death.

Djezahirli was a friend and banker of the Grand-Vizier and reformer Reshid Pasha, former Ottoman Ambassador to Paris, whose protection he enjoyed.

Megerdich Amira Djezahirli (1805–1861)

He supervised the customs' duties of the Empire, a function that no Christian had occupied before him.* He placed 20,000 Armenian employees in the sectors that he controlled. He was above all very keen on progress and knew that it would come from Europe. His great project was teaching in the western style and not according to traditional standards then practised in the East. This inevitably resulted in a conflict with the "old heads," an Armenian expression for the old establishment.

He took particular care over the renovation (1836–1838) of the Nersessian College of Haskeoy, which he entrusted to a brilliant group of teachers, who were responsible, in particular and for the first time, for teaching French and Italian. He invited other Amiras to come and admire this revolutionary establishment. Speeches were given in Armenian, French and Italian. A poem praised the importance of education and a spectacle was shown by the light of magic lanterns, after which the Amiras declared that the school taught magic and accused Megerdich Amira of patronizing impiety and foreign languages.

Devastated by such negative criticism, Megerdich Amira ceased to take an interest in the Nersessian College, which had promised to be so brilliant, but stagnated so quickly.

* With the exception of Ohannes Amira Yerganian, who only obtained the post after he converted to Islam.

The Amira then concentrated his attention on a still more ambitious programme, out of the reach of his enemies. He inaugurated and financed the visit of numerous young Armenians of all social classes to complete their education in French schools and universities. Not enough homage can be paid to the simplicity of this undertaking, the Amira's main claim to fame, resulting in a whole generation of young men who were to breathe new life into Armenia.*

Djezahirli had been a precursor of many other developments in Turkey. For example, in 1850, he had a theatre built in Haskeoy, the first one in Turkey. Unfortunately, this theatre was later demolished by Djezahirli's opponents. Nevertheless, because of Djezahirli, Armenian actors were to achieve international fame – a fact acknowledged even by present day Turks.

This exceptional Amira died in 1861 when he was still in the prime of life. The funeral speech was made by the future Patriarch Nerses Varjabedian who spoke on "*Ounaynoutioune ounaynoutianz.*"† No trace remains of his burial place today.

---

* Among the students was the future Krikor Effendi Agathon (1825–1868), the first Armenian to be named a Minister of the Ottoman Government, where he was given the portfolio of the Ministry of Works. He was in France when he heard of the nomination. He immediately boarded a ship at Marseilles and had scarcely returned to Constantinople where he died before assuming his post.

† *Vanitas Vanitatum.*

From Empire to Republic or the History of a Genocide

Independence at the Price of Blood

Will the history of the Amiras enable one, as some people think, to establish a cause and effect link between their influence and the origin of the genocide of Armenians?

We, for out part, consider those who argue so to be completely wrong. The power and wealth of the Amiras certainly irritated Turks, arousing their anger and jealousy of Christians in whom they only saw enemies of the Faith and parasites of the State, but those times were over.

It is important to recall, in this context, that the power of the Amiras was at its peak in the first half of the 19th century, when the Sultans nicknamed Armenia the "faithful nation," an audacious description since it was "infidel" for Islam, though its loyalties and abilities were appreciated and exploited by successive Sultans.

The grievances, economic as much as religious, against Armenians, ended up finding a sympathetic ear in high places and even an accomplice with the arrival of Abdul-Hamid II who mounted the throne in 1876 – fifteen years or so after the final demise of the Amiras. The "Red Sultan" differed from his predecessors by establishing a climate of terror in Armenia.

Here are two examples of the changes that were taking place.

A Very Promising Evening

In Constantinople, on the evening of February 16th 1907, Artin Effendi Aslan, the only Armenian top civil servant of the Ottoman navy* and his wife, a descendant of the Momdjian Amiras, were giving a reception at their home in Pera, an elegant district of the capital. They were inaugurating a formula that was to influence their prewar receptions. It concerned amateur theatricals borrowed from French tradition and performed in French by their three young daughters. On this occasion they were to act comedies by a fashionable author and mime animated scenes inspired by Cinderella.

The town house of the Aslans, unusual in height and depth, had only a narrow frontage on the small Alleon street and was close to other residences.

* As a civilian he had the title of Rear-Admiral.

The ground floor consisted of a dining room and smoking room, situated each side of a staircase that led to the drawing rooms on the first floor, large enough to accommodate the show and the audience. On these occasions the mistress of the house stood at the top of the stairs and her husband at the bottom, where he not only welcomed the guests, but also walked up the stairs with each new arrival to his wife. Then he walked down again. On that evening they were expecting around a hundred guests.

The Aslans had had the unfortunate idea of inviting the notorious Madame Keushe Oghlou, a dominant woman who was called *Takouk Doudou* – literally Madame the Queen. But that queen was a great sinner. For inexplicable reasons she had been the mistress of Abdul-Hamid, although he had ruined her husband. She had had a daughter and a son from her liaison with the Sultan. The daughter, Astine Gumushguerdan, was the image of her father, physically, but, thank God, not morally. The son, Andon, also resembled his father, not physically, but morally. He was a nasty person, dedicated to serving the Hamidan police as their spy. When he learnt that his mother was invited to Artin Effendi's house that evening, he decided to prevent her from going at all costs. He thought, certain as he was of his impunity, that the best way of achieving this – and at the same time to sow trouble in Christian high-society – was simply to forbid the party. The police were instructed to act accordingly. They invaded the office of Artin Effendi to inform him of the Sultan's wish and give the order, not only to cancel the party, but to ascribe the cancellation to a sudden illness of one of their children.

Artin Effendi knew that it was useless to resist and hurried home to take the necessary steps. His wife, not noticing his pallor, clumsily enquired whether he was planning to wear a dinner jacket or a stambouline (evening frock coat) for the occasion. "Neither one nor the other," he replied in a tired voice. "There will be no party." "Come now," replied Madame Aslan, "it's too late to joke." But she had to face the facts. Then began a race against time. Their eldest daughter, Hermine, fifteen years old, managed to scribble in a few minutes a great many notes cancelling the party. Then all the servants of the house were mobilized, from the butler to the pastry-cook's boy, to ensure that the cancellations were made. Their mission completed, a close member of the family turned up at the Aslan's house. "Artin Effendi," he said, "what's this story about a sick child? Your house is entirely surrounded by police who prevent anyone from entering" and then added a final detail which gave a picturesque touch to the absurdity of the situation, "It is thanks to the shape of my headgear* and the possession of my American nationality that I was able to pass the barriers."

The Strange Encounter of the Two Most Touchy Noses in History. Among so many incredible situations the prize for the most absurd must be awarded to the prominent actor of the Comédie Française, the great Coquelin Cadet, who came to perform Cyrano de Bergerac on the shores of the Bosphorus at the start of the 20th century.

Coquelin was confronted with the most extravagant situation that the Hamidian persecution mania could create. On landing he was taken in hand by the head of censorship who, even in such a delicate position, happened to be an innocent Armenian – simply a loyal civil servant – a descendant of Bedros Amira Brounsouz, who bore the flamboyant name of Minas Effendi Brounsouz-Gamsar.

Coquelin caused Minas Effendi great misgivings at the idea of seeing the actor create a State uproar when declaiming the tirade against Cyrano's nose and its famous proportions. Why such anxiety? Because the nose of Abdul-Hamid was very long and very large. It was the despair of the owner and the joy of his enemies. Henceforth, any allusion to a prominent nose was seen throughout the Empire as an offence and repressed as a crime of *lèse-majesté.*

Fortunately for him, the head of censorship was called "without a nose": *Brounsouz,* literally "noseless" in Turkish. Perhaps he owed his office to his name, if indeed he thought he owed to providence a function that caused him more worry than satisfaction. His position was all the more uncomfortable because he was charged personally with the censorship of the Armenian press. He spent most of his time reassuring the Sultan about the journalists whose writing he did his best to cover, despite the fact that he was supervised by his counter-censors, Turkish and Armenian, for better control of the truth in his reports. The early death of Minas the Noseless is scarcely a surprise!

The Hamidian police system was considered to be one of the best informed in the world and the most odious, like its master.

However that may be, the censor nursed his illusions. Coquelin was the best interpreter of Cyrano de Bergerac, the masterpiece by Edmond

* It was a "European" hat which only foreigners were allowed to wear. The Ottomans and their subjects were obliged to wear a fez.

Rostand. It was therefore inappropriate to even think of altering the text. Minas Effendi learnt this at his cost as soon as he asked Coquelin to skip the dangerous tirade.

"You are not serious, Monsieur, it's a joke," said Coquelin indignantly.

"It's a matter beyond our control," pleaded Minas.

"You could have warned me."

"Alas, the subject is taboo."

"It's a crazy story!"

"It's a question of life or death…"

"You are quite right," exclaimed Coquelin innocently, "a Cyrano without a nose is a Cyrano who has no reason to exist."

"All one can do now is to sacrifice a *raison d'être* for a *raison d'Etat*" murmured the censor very proud of his expression.

"In any case," declared the actor, "Cyrano had no doubt a large nose but a flawless one: that of your master, Sir, has more nose than intuition."

Minas continued to hope, but that was a lack of understanding of what has always made the greatness of artists: resistance to pressure from above. When he heard Coquelin in the heat of the moment attack the fatal passage, he reacted violently. Overriding all restraint, he leapt to the stage, watched by an astonished audience and shouted at Coquelin in a manner unusual for him but which gave an insight concerning the regime, "You wretch, my life is in your hands!" Coquelin bowed "It is better to sacrifice a text than a head, be it that of the censor," he said to himself.

Abdul-Hamid, on hearing of this affair, compensated Coquelin by granting him a decoration. He sowed medals as bribes.

Now let us turn to the second part of this picture which deals with the cruel character of the Hamidian era and the inconceivable paradoxes accompanying imperial cruelty.

Abdul-Hamid's reign coincided with the start of the Russo-Turkish war of 1877-78 which ended with a Russian victory enabling them to by-pass the Bosphorus and Dardanelles Straits. Thus Russia had gained access to the Mediterranean by controlling the Bulgarian port of Dedeagach (Alexandroupolis) though it was denied possession of the Straits.

It was then that Arakel Bey Dadian was officially made responsible for welcoming the Grand Duke Nicholas and an international Armenia was established. The event displeased Sultan Abdul-Hamid who was already ill-disposed towards Armenians.

It was also at that time that Bismarck convened the famous Congress of Berlin with the aim of halting the Russian advance. Europe then forced the Russians to withdraw from Ottoman territories and preserved much of the Ottoman Empire. Great Britain obtained the island of Cyprus from Turkey as part of the deal, while Russia was denied direct access to the Mediterranean.

As for the Armenian Patriarch of Constantinople, he considered that he should be represented at the Congress by a delegation that requested internal autonomy for Armenia in eastern Turkey. As soon as he heard of such a project, Nubar Pasha did all he could to make Mgr. Nerses Varjabedian reconsider his decision. "I am," pointed out the great man, "the only Armenian who can negotiate with the Turks." Nubar knew what he was saying. Had he not been the one who had succeeded in obtaining from the Sublime Porte all the privileges granted to the viceroys of Egypt, theoretically still its vassal? He was therefore on good terms with Ottoman Sultans and much appreciated by them.

Unfortunately it was to no avail. The Armenian intelligentsia and the Patriarch of Constantinople remained adamant – they saw Nubar as a stranger whose prestige irritated them. They sent a delegation to Berlin of inexperienced men, carrying little weight, who failed in their endeavours. They merely exasperated Abdul-Hamid. Nubar Pasha was dismayed, as were Prince Malcom and Count Loris-Melikov, who also attended the Congress.

Another disillusion awaited Nubar. Bismarck dubbed him "the wily little Armenian." Perhaps the Chancellor, on this occasion, was taking stock of himself? Be that as it may, he appreciated Nubar to the point of offering him the throne of Bulgaria, recently freed by the Russians. But the Tsar vetoed the project which had, however, been approved by Europe. The Russians feared the Slavonic little brother becoming a plaything of the Germans.

As for the future "Red Sultan," he considered the question of Armenian autonomy as nothing less than treason, which was later aggravated by the appearance of Armenian revolutionaries and the start of peasant rebellions. This was going too far for the tyrant who would stop at nothing to terrorise not only the handful of agitators but also all of their co-religionists.

Thus it was that at the end of the 19th century three hundred thousand Armenians were killed, leading the British Prime Minister, William Gladstone, to call Abdul-Hamid the "Red Sultan," while Anatole France called the Turkish ruler the "Great Bleeder" with a play on words in French between *Grant Seigneur* and *Grand Saigneur*. Europe was fully aware of the Armenian tragedy but was hostile to any division of the Ottoman Empire that profited the Russians.

Agop Pasha Kazazian (1833–1891)

The Hamidian hatred of Armenia was accompanied by extraordinary inconsistencies and paradoxes. Several Armenian Ministers – who had nothing to do with the revolutionaries – were appointed by Hamid himself to some of the highest and most sensitive posts of Ottoman government. Such appointments may have been homage to Armenian intelligence and competence, but they also doomed them to an increasingly intolerable position. Three Armenian dignitaries, Agop Pasha Kazazian, Mikael Pasha Portugal and Ohannes Pasha Sarkis – the last two Catholics – succeeded each other during Abdul-Hamid's reign as head of the Ministry of the Private Treasury (Finance Ministry) whose incumbents took precedence over other ministers and, according to Ottoman protocol, ranked just below the Grand-Vizier.

One of the most influential of these Armenians, Artin Pasha Dadian (1830–1901), was the son of Ohannes Amira Dadian, Under-secretary of State for Foreign Affairs, who headed Ottoman diplomacy during the last quarter of the 19th century. An excellent servant of the Empire and the Nation, one of his chief merits was trying to conciliate Hamidian terror with the protection of Armenia. He deployed great skill in avoiding the worst when Armenian revolutionaries occupied the Ottoman Bank in 1896.

More disconcerting was the fact, attested by the best Turkish sources,* that Abdul-Hamid – like Hitler who is said to have had a Jewish mother –

* Ali Kemal Meram, *Padisah Analari* [The Mothers of the Sultans], Istanbul: Toplumsal Dönüsüm Yayinlari, 1997.

had an Armenian mother called Virginie, a native of Russia. She had been the preferred favourite of Abdul-Medjid and had given him a son, Abdul-Hamid. Thus the most charming of Sultans fathered the most odious tyrant. During the reign of Hamid, the first lady of the Empire, the Sultana Validé, was Armenian, the only one to have given birth to an Ottoman Sultan.

In this connection it is worth referring to what is said in the diary (kept in beautiful French) and cherished by one of Arakel Bey Dadian's granddaughters. Araxia Vahan-Gulbenkian was a young interpreter at the royal court who translated for the Sultans what was said to them in the language of Molière by the European Princesses received at Constantinople.

The most interesting passage of the diary was written when the Emperor and Empress of Germany visited Turkey in 1889. The young interpreter had recently started at the Imperial Palace and drew an unflattering portrait of the Validé:

> All of a sudden, they came to tell me that her Highness, the Validé Sultana, had asked for me. I rose at once and tried to remember all the beautiful phrases and all the recommendations that Papa had given me. I approached her, went down on one knee and bowed a little, thinking she was going to stop me. But when I realized that such was not her intention, I waved at her and got up. The Validé Sultana is a small old lady whose age one cannot tell exactly. She has fair hair, a shiny face with red cheeks, rather short, wearing the Turkish costume which consists of a sort of indoor dress with a large jacket floating around her waist. Her head is covered with a veil with diamonds and at the front, a bird's feather surmounted with large emeralds of the most beautiful purity.

The narrator then continues her account:

> After half an hour, during which I practised curtseying in front of a mirror, I was called for again. This time, apart from the Validé Sultana, I found myself in the presence of the Princesses Zekiye, Nahimiye and Nahile, aged 18, 13 and the third 7 (...). The Validé Sultana again asked some questions and then I left. It must have been 9 or perhaps 10 o'clock when the Empress arrived (...) followed by his Majesty the Sultan (...). Suddenly I heard the Sultan pronounce my name and Madame Hobé Pasha came towards me (...). With a firm step I followed her. On passing in front of our sovereign I made a deep bow with my hand and approached the Empress. Madame Hobé spoke some words in German to her, pointing at me, while I made a deep curtsey and was astonished, and

> at the same time confused, when I saw her Majesty rise and hold out her hand to me. Despite my emotion I kept my head, shook her hand and curtseyed a second time. '*Sprechen Sie deutsch?*'* she asked. '*Sehr wenig Majestät*'† I replied. '*Wo haben Sie abgelernt?*'‡ '*Hier in Constantinopolis, Majestät*'**
>
> The short dialogue over, the Empress sat down. Then the Validé, pulling my arm, ordered me to say to her Majesty how happy she was to have made her acquaintance (…). Finally the Validé Sultana said to me: 'Please ask her Majesty to speak French.'
>
> On hearing this order I was astounded and thinking I had not understood properly, I asked her to repeat the phrase. She said the same thing. I found myself obliged to express Her Highness' desire to the Empress. 'Do you understand French?' asked her Majesty (to the Validé)?' 'One or two words' said the Validé in Turkish, suiting the action to the word. I translated one or two more insignificant phrases (…). After twenty minutes Her Majesty rose begging to leave. She left giving her arm to the Sultan followed by her ladies-in-waiting. When she had disappeared I saw the Validé raise her arms to heaven as if to give thanks to God murmuring, 'Bouda bitdi' [*this too is over*] (…) I turned my heels and slipped away for fear of Her Highness noticing that I had heard her exclamation…

One can note that given the silence of Araxia on this subject, the Yildiz Palace hushed up the Armenian origin of this Highness who, moreover, did not seem to have been very bright.

In 1908 the Committee of Union and Progress, a hot-bed of those who were euphemistically called "Young Turks," seized power. Helped by Armenian revolutionaries, they ended the reign of the Red Sultan but not his hatred of Armenia, which they adopted and carried to its climax. The Armenian revolutionaries realized that they had been duped.

The Young Turks did not dare to inform the Sultan in person of his dethronement but called upon representatives of the non-Muslim minorities to do the job for them. Eram Effendi Eramian, a Catholic Armenian from Erzeroum, a life senator of the Empire, was asked to head the delegation responsible for the dismissal of the Sultan.

---

* Do you speak German?

† Very little, Majesty.

‡ Where did you learn it?

** Here in Constantinople, Majesty.

Four men clad in black were then seen arriving at the Yildiz Palace and asking to see the Sultan. The Armenian dignitary advanced at the head of a delegation, preceding a Greek Pasha and a Jewish Pasha side by side, followed by a very small Turkish Pasha who, trembling, brought up the rear. When the four members of the delegation were in the presence of the man who had made Turkey tremble for thirty years, they were surprised to see a humble and docile man, a "Great Lord," his nose more hooked than ever, bowing before infidels and leaving his palace without a word.

Reassured, the Young Turks then showed their true nature, spreading fear and advocating extreme nationalism, panturkism, and hatred for Armenians – as the 1909 massacre of Armenians in Adana (Cilicia) paved the way for the genocide of 1915. From 1913 the Young Turks placed the government of the Empire under the dictatorial authority of a Triumvirate: Talaat Pasha at the Interior Ministry, Enver Pasha at the War Ministry, and Djemal Pasha at the Navy.

Thus Turkey watched the outbreak of war in 1914 between the Triple Entente (France, England, and Russia) and the Central Powers (Germany and Austro-Hungary). Italy soon joined the Entente and Turkey the Central Powers.

Then the Triumvirate, Germany's ally and accomplice, wanted to profit from the conditions created by the world conflict to put an end to Armenia and they gave the signal for a genocide on April 24th 1915 starting with the annihilation of the Armenian intelligentsia of Constantinople (doctors, writers, lawyers...) which claimed several hundred victims among the intellectual elite of the Nation. This was followed by the methodical extermination of the population, not only in eastern Anatolia but also in central Anatolia under the grotesque pretext that Armenia was preparing to hand over Turkey to Russia.

That Russophiles existed in Ottoman Armenia was not surprising, but the majority of Armenians in Turkey remained loyal to Turkey. Therefore, the martyrdom of Armenia appears not only to be a crime but a fault, an unmotivated error, and all the more detestable.

The profound reasons for the carnage lay elsewhere. They were rooted in the racial illusion of a Pan-Turanian empire, bringing together, under Ottoman rule, all the Turcophone populations from the Bosphorus to the borders of China. Conceivable in the absolute despite its extremism – and still topical for some Turks – such a dream was cherished by Enver Pasha, the Young Turk Minister of War for whom the Armenian nation had to be eliminated since it constituted, by its race and faith, the only non-indigenous obstacle to the "homogeneity" of an empire which was to extend from one end of Asia to the other.

In such a context it is clear that no link existed between the power of the Amiras and the cause of the genocide.

If Enver was the instigator of the carnage, Talaat was the organizer, while Djemal's role seems less clear. It was Talaat who ordered provincial governors by coded telegram to carry out extermination. It is therefore he who is considered the prime executioner of the genocide and it was to him that, dismayed by the news coming from Anatolia, Armenian dignitaries of Constantinople turned. They had been spared as high civil servants of the Empire but were determined to take all possible steps to halt the bloodshed. We shall mention four.

1. Ohannes Pasha Kouyoumdjian, last Christian governor of Ottoman Lebanon, burst into the smartest club of the capital, a favourite meeting-place of the Young Turk Pashas, where he said in a thundering voice, "What does this news from Anatolia mean?" How did the Turkish Pashas react? They all silently turned their backs on the intruder.

2. Eram Effendi Eramian – whom the Young Turks had made responsible for the dismissal of Abdul-Hamid – learning about the murder of his family in Erzeroum, ran to the Triumvirate to demand an explanation. "We did not know" said Talaat, Enver and Djemal all together. "Why did you not give us their names, we would have given orders that they be spared." "I did not know that you were assassins," replied Eram before resigning his post as a life senator.

3. Abraham Pasha Karakehia, octogenarian and holding back his tears with difficulty, went to see Talaat to exhort him to put an end to the carnage. His interlocutor interrupted him saying, "Pasha, think of your *keif* (pleasure) without meddling in such affairs."

4. Manoug Effendi Azarian, life senator, former Ambassador of the Empire to Belgrade and Bucharest, former President of the Mixed European Commission on the Danube, also tried to intervene with Talaat and entreat him to condemn only those who were guilty and to spare a population whose innocence was certainly known to the Minister of the Interior. "I haven't time to dally with such details," answered the killer who ended the interview with this terrible remark, "The same water will wash them all."*

Aware of their helplessness, the last Armenian dignitaries of the Empire abandoned their functions and their beloved city and set out for France, their spiritual home. From 1922 they also faced the vengeance of the Kemalists who stole their properties and banished their owners.

But the nostalgia of the Bosphorus and its palaces never left them… this Bosphorus which for nearly three hundred years had exerted an immense power of fascination on the Amiras.

May the present author be permitted to pay tribute to Tsar Ferdinand of Bulgaria whom Turkey, in 1915, asked for the "repatriation" of Bulgarian Armenians to submit them to the same fate as Turkish Armenians. The Tsar, albeit an ally of Turkey during the Great War, refused to comply with this request. Tsar Ferdinand's Armenian subjects were eternally grateful, as testified to the author by senior officers, industrial magnates and others, when he was an attache of the French Embassy at Sofia.

Before the 1917 revolution ended, the Russian armies of Nicolas II had penetrated eastern Turkey, supported by Armenian volunteers from Russia. Horrified by the genocide, many volunteers were impatient to retaliate against Turks and Kurds. Led by their famous General Antranig, they won some battles but did not kill one or two million Turks as Kemalist propaganda claimed.

On October 30th 1918 the Ottoman Empire capitulated at Mudros. The Allies entered Constantinople and the question of the genocide was immediately addressed. The new Turkish government of a dying empire for the first time in history included four Armenian ministers and admitted the reality of the Armenian massacres for which a Court Martial was set up in 1919. These Turkish courts found the previous leaders of Turkey – who had fled the country – guilty and sentenced them to death.

It is important to note that Ottoman authorities at this time admitted the reality of the extermination. The denial of the massacres came later.

Some Armenians took the law into their hands. A national hero, son of genocide victims, Soghomon Tehlirian, shot dead, in a Berlin street, Talaat Pasha, the great organizer of the massacres. A German court acquitted the Armenian. Twenty years later, Talaat's remains were solemnly brought back to Turkey and the Turkish President inaugurated the statue in Istanbul in Talaat's glorious memory.

---

* A Turkish proverb meaning "All will have the same fate and the same death."

Djemal was also executed by an Armenian in Tiflis in 1922. As for Enver, always chasing his pan-Turkish pipe-dream, he was killed in 1922, reportedly by a Soviet Armenian. Brought back in 1996, his remains were given the same honour as those of Talaat.

Today Turkish officials desperately deny the genocide. They pretend to see a personal insult in the slightest allusion to it. There are thousands of examples. Let us give but one: Ohannes Gulbenkian (1895–1986), great-grandson of Arakel Bey Dadian, considered a Turcophile, gave lunch in the spring of 1955 at a good Parisian restaurant, in honour of the Consul General of Turkey and Madame Dyarbekirian, descendant of an ancient family of Smyrna and married to an Argentinian Armenian millionaire. During the meal, Madame Dyarbekirian brought the conversation onto the massacres. Indignant, the Turk rose and stormed out of the restaurant. After reproaching the beautiful guest, who burst out laughing for her "lack of tact," Ohannes Gulbenkian insisted on giving his own version of the genocide, evoked, should one say, in the manner of an Oriental narrative, just like the personage. Here, in substance, is what he told us:

Early in the spring of 1915, when he had just turned twenty, Ohannes was riding on horseback along the alleyways of Kadikeoy,* when he noticed that his horse suddenly began to limp. At the same time he saw another rider coming towards him. Without waiting for him, Ohannes dismounted to look for the cause of his horse's trouble. Before he had made the discovery, the stranger, coming alongside, also dismounted and said, "Can I help you?" Suiting the action to the word with a quick look, he removed a small stone from the animal's painful limb. The two men became friendly. The stranger was a handsome Circassian, like all Circassians. He was called Hassan *Cherkess* ("Circassian" in Turkish) and was an officer of the Imperial Navy and principal private secretary to Djemal Pasha who had just informed him that the Triumvirate had taken the decision to massacre the Armenians. Djemal also added that Hassan was going to be appointed Director of the refugee camps. "Oh *Pasham!*"† implored the Circassian, "I cannot sully my hands in this way." "But no, wait!" replied Djemal, "It is not a question of sullying your hands but of saving lives. If you save fifty condemned people, it will be as many men saved." His mother, having said the same thing, Hassan agreed to play the game. On arrival at his destination, he did his best

* A suburb of Constantinople on the Asian shore.

† Pasham (*Ott. Tur.*): My Pasha.

to bungle the orders received, with the discrete help of the Ministry of the Navy.

This is what Ohannes wished to prove. He concluded his explanation in these terms, "If Enver and Talaat were abominable assassins, Djemal was less evil than them."

Hassan Cherkess was not the only person who saved Armenian lives. Several highly-placed Turkish officials – provincial governors and mayors of large towns – had the courage to refuse to carry out the orders of extermination and paid for their generosity by being ruined or even killed. Nor can one forget those Turkish families who sheltered numerous orphans whom they snatched from death by converting them to Islam.

On the other hand, and always with a desire for historical objectivity, it should be said that, not content with killing their victims, the murderers followed the physical genocide of Armenians with a cultural and religious genocide, systematically destroying all Armenian churches and monasteries they encountered...

Ohannes Gulbenkian continued his narrative. Relating the events of 1919, he said that after the capitulation of the Empire he was summoned by the Grand-Vizier, who said, "*Oghloum*,[*] I appeal to you as a descendant of a noble family famous for its loyalty to the Empire and its fidelity to its Sultans. Before informing the commanders of the Allied forces, I should like to see you carry out an opinion-poll among the chief Armenian dignitaries of Constantinople to learn their views concerning the creation in Cilicia of an Armenian Principality which would be autonomous and placed under the nominal authority of a member of the Imperial family. I wish you to do this very secretly." The Grand-Vizier was evidently aware that between the 11th and 14th centuries Cilicia had been the seat of a flourishing Armenian kingdom.

Despite the condition of secrecy given by Damad Ferid Pasha, Ohannes made the mistake of confiding in Zaven Patriarch, although the latter was known to be a controversial prelate and did not hold his tongue. Next morning a dozen Armenian revolutionaries burst into Ohannes' house and, daggers in hand, said to him, "Turcophilia, sir, is a crime." The servants of the young Bey quickly shielded their master with their bodies and thrust the intruders out. Sometime later, the Grand-Vizier was overthrown, as was his project. Much to the joy of Armenians, Cilicia was given to France! But,

* Oghlouom (*Ott. Tur.*): My son.

alas! Our country, sick of war, failed to defend Cilicia when the Kemalist troops attacked it.

Miraculously for his country, Mustafa Kemal snatched Turkey from disintegration. He was a nationalist like the Young Turks whose policies he adopted in order to complete the genocide before becoming its chief denier. As soon as he came to power he abolished not only the Sultanate and its Armenian minority, but he declared null and void the verdict of the Ottoman Courts Martial. No doubt considering the genocide to be a disgrace to Turkey in the face of the outside world, he resolved to bury the shame deep in the bowels of the young republic, preferring guilty silence over integrity.

It would be unjust to consider all Turks as assassins as it would be absurd to confuse Naziism with all Germans. Indeed, by their tolerance, the true Osmanlis were superior beings. But one cannot overlook the horror of a Turkish policy which did not stop at the Armenian genocide but followed it in 1922 with a Greek genocide and in 1930s a Kurdish genocide.

In this connection it would be difficult to recall the Armenian genocide without mentioning the part played by Kurdish mercenaries hired by the Young Turk government. The responsibility for the deeds of these mercenaries cannot fall on all Kurds who still endure today a form of genocide due to Turkish military operations in south-eastern Anatolia. It is thus that more than half of the Kurds of Turkey have had to evacuate to the suburbs of large Turkish towns or flee to Western Europe, thus forming a new diasprora.

An Independent Armenia

Profiting by the collapse of Imperial Russia, a short-lived and fragile Armenia came into being between 1918 and 1920 in former Armenian lands of the Russian Empire. Its governors, coming from various backgrounds, realized that, in order to give Armenia a semblance of stability, they should call upon the descendants of Amiras as the most suitable to provide the necessary panache. It was thus that Tigrane Chaïan was appointed as a representative to Athens, Diran Noradounghian to Rome (the Vatican), Charles Sarkis to London, and Boghos Nubar Pasha to Paris, where he headed the Armenian delegation at the Peace Conference.

However, this grand display of diplomacy was of no practical use. Armenia bore the cost of a situation which was beyond its control, as Bolsheviks and Kemalists conspired in her fall under the domination of the USSR which, at that time, offered the only bastion against Turkish covetousness. Armenia therefore became a Soviet Republic.

Seventy years later, profiting by the collapse of the USSR, the small Soviet Republic of Armenia proclaimed its independence on September 21st 1991. Let us quickly look at the destiny of Armenia in terms of the constraints weighing on its present policy.

Scarcely free, Armenia was confronted with great dangers for having courageously answered the appeal of its compatriots in Nagorno-Karabagh (Artsakh) to be united with their mother-land. Karabagh had always been Armenian and only a Machiavellian calculation by Stalin had included it in Muslim and Turkic Azerbaijan. The occupation of Karabagh by the Azeris was at best legal without being legitimate.

Thus, from the start, independence condemned Armenia to war with an Azerbaijan determined to keep Karabagh at all costs. Turkey was all too happy to support its blood-brother to crush the nascent Armenian state.

Azeris believe Karabagh to be Azeri in the way that Turks believe that the Armenian Genocide never took place. In this context, however, Armenia managed to snatch Karabagh from the Azeris. Then, in 1993, the government of Ankara sent a scarcely veiled threat to Yerevan of military intervention. Facing such a threat, Armenia was able to rely on the help, discrete but vital, of other neighbours who were rivals with Turkey. These were initially Russia, which backed Armenia militarily, but also Iran, which supported her materially. Turkey withdrew.

But a reversal of the situation is always possible and Armenia must never forget that its position remains a vulnerable one because of Turco-Azeri hostility and the absence of oil (or oil pipelines) in its territory. These factors could lead to outside powers losing interest in Armenia's fate. What would become of Armenia then?

While cultivating defensive alliances, Yerevan should also make overtures to Turkey. Armenian leaders must know, in this context, that it has at its disposal an ultimate weapon that could be used wisely. This weapon is none other than that of the Genocide, which becomes a key asset if it is used as a means and not as an end. Like a block of stone, Turkey refuses desperately to admit its heinous crime. It is up to Armenia to know how to skirt the rock rather than be dashed against it. What is most important for Yerevan is to make Turkey yield without a head-on clash. In this respect, Armenia is in greater need of consideration by the world, than of charity from the Turks. The universal recognition of the Armenian Genocide is on the right track. As this circle enlarges, Turkey has to climb down.

Armed with the genocide, Armenia can even bear pressure on outside powers as much as, if not more, than Turkey. With regard to the Turks, the genocide should not be mummified but used to obtain the lifting of the scandalous blockade imposed by Ankara on Armenia since the beginning of the Karabagh war, and the formal unification of this same Karabagh to its mother-country. Let us repeat, the essential element remains the international recognition of the genocide. With this in view, Armenia should be satisfied by the recognition of the Genocide by the European Parliament in 1987, Russia in 1995, Greece in 1996, Belgium in 1998, and finally, by France on May 29th 1998.

The gesture of France bestows a new dimension on the Armenian question. Not only does it show the path it proposes to be followed, but it marks the point of no return. The other great powers will inevitably follow suit. It is a good occasion for Armenia to render solemn homage to France, which has been the main asylum in Europe for the survivors of the Genocide, resulting today in the existence of a flourishing Franco-Armenian community, 400,000 strong. One of the main centres of a diaspora with over a million Armenians is the United States, with as many in Russia, 250,000 in Lebanon, 140,000 in Iran, 100,000 in Canada, 100,000 in Argentina etc... If one adds to these figures the 3,750,000 inhabitants of Armenia itself, one can say that the total number of Armenians in the world is around 6-7 million, half in Armenia, half in the diaspora.

Today, Armenia is at a cross-road. It has an appointment with the future. Better than anyone, it knows that, owing to its geographical position and history, Armenians and Turks will have to get on together to ensure the harmony of the Caucasus and guarantee the prosperity promised by the oil of the Caspian Sea. These possibilities are heightened because there seem to be significant changes on the Turkish side of the border. These changes have been modest, but promising, since they are militating in favour of recognition of the historical truth and reconciliation.

It is up to Armenian diplomacy to know how to exploit the capital of sympathy it enjoys throughout the world, in order to help it overcome the blockades inherited from the past and to establish, with Turkey, a *modus vivendi,* which would suffice to make Azerbaijan ponder.

In any case, Armenia would not be the sole beneficiary of a rapprochement with Ankara, which would gain advantages by consenting to a "reconciliation" whose first effect would be the improvement of its public image beyond its frontiers.

A final remark needs to be made concerning the recognition of the Genocide: a difference of interpretation exists between the Armenian diaspora and Yerevan. The former engages the issue with passion, Yerevan considers it with reason. The explanation is simple: the Armenians of the Russia Empire were spared the carnage of 1915, whereas those of the diaspora are its direct outcome.

One cannot complete a review of Armenia's neighbours without mentioning Georgia – a Christian Georgia, like Armenia – whose courage and pride have never failed in the course of the centuries during which both countries were strongholds of Christianity in the Caucasus. Everything should bring them together but a curious reticence* weighs on their relationship despite the fact that two branches of the same dynasty, that of the Bagratids, had reigned over both countries since the early Middle Ages (in Armenia up to 1064 or the Sejuk invasions, and in Georgia until 1801, the date of its union with Russia). It is obvious that the two states must maintain good relations in line with their common past greatness and their present mutual responsibilities.

---

* Here too one must seek its origin in the divergences of a confessional nature, Georgia having succumbed to Byzantine Orthodoxy, unlike Armenia.

Epilogue

Paris July 1945

Just after the Second World War, in 1945 – I was then seventeen – I remembered on a Saturday afternoon that a poetess was to recite some of her poems at the Nubarian Library.* I arrived there at the indicated time and found the door shut. In front of the door stood a man of great bearing, wearing a bowler hat, which he removed upon seeing me. Bowing to him, I asked politely if there was any hope of seeing the door opening and the arrival of the poetess. "*Haygagan anganonoutioun*"† grumbled this great man who was still unknown to me. Calming down, he asked for my name. "I am," I replied with the pride I have always had, "the grandson of Madam Artin Effendi Aslan." He then related to me with a respect that still makes me blush.

We understood each other at once, and we engaged, as one, in a dialogue whose substance and elegance made it one of the best memories of my youth. As we were about to part, after a fruitless wait of thirty minutes – which had seemed only five to me – this exceptional person took leave saying, "Kindly pay my respects to Madame, your grandmother, on behalf of Tigrane Chaïan."

No sooner said than done. I then learnt that I had met a descendant of Varteres Amira Chayents (1722–1799), an ex-Ottoman diplomat and then Armenian Ambassador in Athens from 1918 to 1920.

Some years after that encounter that is still in my dreams, the same lordly person was found wandering on waste ground, owing to the inexorable loss of his means of existence. Fortunately for him, he died a few days later. I can still hear Princess Victoria Malcom saying to me, "How distinguished he was."

***

On finishing this book I must admit that as far as I am concerned, I have no illusions. Nearly forty years ago, when I was appointed secretary of the French Embassy at Ankara, where I was pleased to serve France in the

* Situated Square Alboni, this Armenian library in Paris was offered to the Nation by Boghos Pasha Nubar.

† "Disorganisation in Armenian style."

country of my roots, I received death threats for no reason. A week after hearing a man's voice on the telephone saying, with a strong accent, "Monsieur, you will be killed," my car burst into flames as I turned on the ignition. I barely had time to get out when I saw my car completely burnt out. People "in the know" said to me, lowering their voices, that "the presence at the French Embassy of a diplomat of Armenian origin was not to the liking of the Turkish authorities…" They added, in a candid tone, that I had been lucky (sic) in so far as Turkey had contented itself with giving me *"a warning and not really death,"* the subtlety being that the car had burnt and not exploded…

No doubt, on reading these pages, Turkish readers may consider me to be a Turcophobe and Armenian readers a Turcophile… yet I am neither one nor the other. Through the facts and the situations that I have evoked, and by the testimonies that I have recorded, I have only wished to be impartial, to snatch from historical oblivion men who do not deserve to be forgotten.

It is possible that present-day Armenians do not recognize the deep Armenian identity of the persons brought alive in these pages, those of the 18th century possibly seeming Turkified and those of the 19th century too Gallicised. If such be the case – as I greatly fear – I cannot repeat often enough that, for the Amiras, obedience to Turkey had been the protective cover to their patronage and French culture the criterion of their grandeur.

Throughout the 20th century, Armenians had generally been depicted, at best, as victims of a genocide, and at worst, as carpet-dealers. My ambition was to show that Armenia was not limited to these extremes: it had also been aristocratic, even if it had not been free. If the hazards of history had made Ottoman Armenia bend under the yoke of an oppressor, the glory and prestige of the Amiras revealed, for a while, its capacity to exert its own supremacy.

Decendants of the Amiras who Shared Their Memories with Me.

Mrs. Edgard Bey Duz, born Allahverdi.
Mrs. Artin Effendi Aslan, born Momdjian.
Miss Duruk Harentz.
Mrs. Gabriel Effendi Servicen, born Vahan, (granddaughter of Arakel Bey Dadian).
Princess Victoria Malcom, (granddaughter of Arakel Bey Dadian).
Mrs. Naguib Pasha Boutros-Ghali, born Aslan, (granddaughter of Ohannes Bey Dadian).
Baroness Sérot-Alméras-Latour, born Eramian.
Mrs. Avilia Stephen, born Topalian, (great grand daughter of Ohannes Bey Dadian).
Miss Anahide Merametdjian.
Diran Bey Noradounghian
Sarkis Bey Duz.
Mr. Ohannes Gulbenkian, (great grand son of Arakel Bey Dadian).
Mr. Leon Enkserdjis.
Mr. Nubar Tavitian, (descendant of Missak Amira).

Bibliography

Adalian, Rouben, "The Armenian Colony of Egypt during the reign of Muhammed Ali," *The Armenian Review*, Boston, 1980.

Alboyadjian, Arshag, *Les Dadians,* Le Claire, 1965.

Alishan, Father Léonce, *Sissouan ou l'Arméno-Cicilie*, Vénise, 1899.

Artinian, Vartan, *A Study of the Historical Development of the Armenian Constitutional System in the Ottoman Empire*, (PhD thesis, Brandeis University, 1970).

Barsoumian, Hargop Levon, *The Armenian Amira Class of Istanbul*, Columbia University, 1980.

Bélédian, Krikor, *Les Arméniens*, Brépols, Paris, 1994.

Berberian, Avedis, *Batmoutioun Hayots*, Constantinople, 1871.

Boghossian, Father Yeprem, *Kouyoumdjian yev Tinguirian Kerstasdanner* [The Kouyoumdjian and Tinguirian Families], Vienna, 1951.

Boghossian, Father Yeprem, *Allahverdian Kertasdan* [The Allahverdi Family], Vienna, 1957.

Boutros-Ghali, Anna, *Les Dadians, Souvenirs de famille*, Cairo, (around 1965)

Commission of the Commérmoration (anonyme), *Barsagan Hishadagaran Yérevman S. Khach yegeghetsvo Kourou Cheshméi,* Istanbul, 1934.

Damad, Marianne, *Souvenirs de famille et d'Orient,* Autun, 1916.

Der Nersessian, Sirarpie, *Armenia and the Byzantine Empire,* Cambridge, Mass. Harvard, 1945.

Jamgocyan, Onnik, Les Finances de l'Empire Ottoman et les financiers de Constantinople (1732-1853) PhD thesis, Paris, 1988.

Kévorkian, Raymond *Revue d'Histoire Arménienne Contemporaine,* Paris, 1995 and 1998.

Menevichian, Father Gabriel, *Azkapanoutioun Aznouvagan Zarmin Duziantz* [Genealogy of the Noble Duz Family], Vienna, 1890.

Meram, Ali Kémal, *Padisah Analari* [The Mothers of Sultans], Istanbul: Toplumsal Dönüsüm Yayinlari, 1997.

Minassian, Jean, *Une Sultane française,* Eugène Figuière, Paris, 1928.

Mirmirian, H. G., *Masnagan Badmoutioun Hay Medzadounnerou* [Monograph of Armenian Maguatess], Constantinople, 1909.

Morery, Louys, *Le Grand Dictionnaire historique,* Amsterdam, 1694.

Morgan, Jacques de, *Histoire du people Arménien,* Berger-Levrault, Paris & Nancy, 1919.

Mouradian, Claire, *L'Arménie,* Presses Universitaires de France, coll. «Que sais-je?», nº 851, Paris, 1996.

Nizamian, Father Kévork, *Parizahay Daretsouyts* [Paris Armenian Almanac], Paris, 1943.

Ohsson, Mouradja d', *Tableau général de l'Empire Ottoman,* Paris, 1987–1820.

Ormanian, Mgr. Maghakia, *Azkabadoum* [History of the Nation], 3 vols., Constantinople, 1913.

Sakisian, Armenag, *Pages d'Art Arménien,* Paris, 1940.

Salaberry, *Histoire de l'Empire Ottoman,* Paris, 1817.

Sevadjian, Marie, *L'Amira,* translated from Armenian by Frédéric Macler, Paris, 1927

Chamchian, Father Mikayel, *Batmoutioun Hayots* [History of Armenians], Venice, 1784–1786.

Tchéraz, Minas, *Guensakragan Miussinner* [Biographical Mosaic], Paris, 1929.

Ter Minassian, Anahide, "L'Arménie et l'éveil des nationalités (1800–1914)" in *Histoire des Arméniens,* published by Gérard Dédéyan, Private, Toulouse, 1982.

Tuglaci, Pars, *The Role of the Balian Family in Architecture,* Istanbul, 1990.

Tuglaci, Pars, *The Role of the Dadian Family in Ottoman Social, Economic and Political Life,* Istanbul,1993.

Ubicini, M. A., *Lettres sur la Turquie,* Paris, 1853.

Urquhart, David, *Turkey and its Resources,* London: Saunders and Otley, 1833.

Vahan-Gulbenkian, Araxia,* *Journal (1888–1892).*

Varjabedian, Father Hagop, *Hishadagaran Hariuramia Hopeliani Haskiughi S. Sdepanos Yegeghetsvo* [Centenary of St. Stepanos Church of Haskeoy], Istanbul, 1931.

Zartarian, Vahan, *Hishadagaran* [Memorial], Constantinople, 1911.

* Grand daughter of Arakel Bey Dadian.

Books on Modern Armenian History

Gomidas Institute
42 Blythe Rd.
London W14 0HA
United Kingdom
www.gomidas.org
info@gomidas.org

Our imprints include Gomidas Institute, Taderon Press, Sterndale Classics and Parvana

Printed in the USA
CPSIA information can be obtained
at www.ICGtesting.com
LVHW041439250124
769628LV00012B/530

9 781903 656358